soul center

JENNIFER RURKA

soul center

THE SEE IT THROUGH METHOD

to take control OF YOUR EMOTIONS, HEAL

YOUR PAST, AND *live a soulful life*

Copyright © 2022 Jennifer Rurka

PUBLISHING

Contact information for White Mud Publishing– jenrurka@hotmail.com

ISBN: 978-1-7782858-3-7 (paperback)
ISBN: 978-1-7782858-0-6 (ebook)

Ordering Information:
Special discounts are available on quantity purchases by corporations, associations, and others. For details, contact jenrurka@hotmail.com

To my tiny little angel and love of my life, Abby
my five-pound Yorkshire terrier. She passed away March 1ˢᵗ 2021

TABLE OF CONTENTS

INTRODUCTION

Before we begin, I want to make something clear. The opinions expressed throughout this book are totally based on my experiences and perspective. This book is my creation, not someone else's. This book contains my original thoughts, and these methods were born out of me through my life's experiences.

As for me, one of my career choices is to facilitate yoga. I have been a certified yoga facilitator for 13 years, which has helped to give me insights into my body and myself. To me, a facilitator is someone who, because of their present state of mind, acts more as a conduit to receive and relay information. Trusting who I am enables me to merge with the class. Then, in that vast openness, I hear the participants requirements.

Today, my primary focus is on coaching clients through the methods I've used to peel back all my layers on this journey of discovery and growth.

I am not a doctor or a therapist, and I'm not instructing you to do anything or advising a product or service for you to buy into. I am simply sharing some of my life with you and some of the techniques I use to coach my clients on their journeys.

I encourage you to pay attention to how you feel when reading this book rather than trying to think it through. Also, notice when you're feeling triggered, because as we will soon discover, this knowledge and awareness is what enables us to know ourselves better.

I will purposely repeat myself in different ways throughout the book to help you remember, rather than forget, because when we are busy being busy, we tend to act like a goldfish, forgetting every three seconds. This book is here to help shine a spotlight on who you're being so that you can see yourself again, and in doing so, help you and those around you to live a more enjoyable life.

Everything is always in motion and becoming something new. Therefore, everything is always beginning.

Chapter 1

THE WHITEOUT

I was 27 years old when I finally hit rock bottom. Following another night of drinking, I'd gone to bed in a drunken stupor and woke up the next morning in physical pain. I had a hurricane headache, no memory of the night before, and weakness and trembling in my body. Sadly, that was the normal part—it was the stabbing pain running down the side of my neck and across my chest that wasn't. I'd never felt such pain before, yet I still neglected to pick up the phone to call for help. Instead, I listened to the dysfunctional part of my brain that told me to *drink the pain away.* And that's what I did, or at least, what I tried to do.

After a few good swigs from the half-empty bottle of schnapps next to me on the couch, it all came back up. At that point, the pain had become so intense that I couldn't even get up to clean myself. Every part of my body felt stiff and heavy, as if I had hundreds of pounds sitting on my chest. Then, without knowing why, I said, "I am having a heart attack, and I'm going to die." As the words left my mouth, another voice that seemed not my own said, "Yes, and that's okay."

I had no idea where the words came from, nor did I care. Oddly, I felt comforted by them. In a way it was like soft cloud arms had wrapped themselves around me—and that's when it happened, everything turned white. There was no couch, no house, no body, no city, no buildings. The mind that I knew, the one that was killing itself, had been emptied out.

In the blink of an eye, there was only white. I could neither see nor feel my body, yet I felt calm. The voices of a man and a woman spoke to me simultaneously, leading me to believe they were one bodyless state of consciousness. Through their words, I could see images. Their words showed me through the eyes of all those that loved me how the alcohol was killing me. Before, it seemed like my immediate family was speaking another language. I couldn't, or wouldn't, hear anyone else's voice but my own. I hated myself so much that I'd left no room for kindness to get in. Now I could not only hear everyone's concerns, but I could feel them too.

At that time, I didn't realize how bad my drinking had become but only because I didn't allow myself to take in its consequences. I hated myself, but what I hated more was thinking about how much I hated myself. Alcohol interceded that for me. It numbed me, and that temporarily permitted me to feel alright in my sickly skin.

The voices told me that I was being given a second chance at life. The message was pure love—a kind of love I had never experienced before, and it was 100% pain free. The love I experienced prior to that day had been filled with heartache. These voices sank deep beneath my skin and into my core, becoming an integral part of the person I would eventually grow into.

I have no immediate recollection of emerging from the whiteout, though my life did begin to drastically change in its aftermath. Once I no longer needed alcohol, my thinking became clearer, and I began seeing people and my environment differently. This is what ultimately led me to new people, places, and situations.

Since cause and effect dictates how we view the world, I didn't feel attracted to the same people that I once did. The birds of a feather flock together, and often through cause and effect. We do not come together by chance—we are vibrational beings that either vibrate towards or away from one another.

As my perception changed, so too did my vibration. I was no longer on the same emotional wavelength as my previous friends. This does not mean that I went to a better place than them. I simply moved into a different mental atmosphere that, regardless of the alcohol, many of us move in and out of daily. Understanding where our thinking can take us is essential and allows us to be more consciously aware of our frame of mind. With the right first step, it's possible to reach a better place mentally and physically.

The SIT Method

Before we go any further, let me first explain what the SIT method is. The SIT method has helped me gain awareness and allowed me the chance to grow and change my perspectives. Everything that happened after the whiteout led me to developing this concept to help myself through difficult times.

This self-help system that I call The SIT method is an abbreviation for *See It Through*. The *it* is a negatively charged belief, while the method is a way of doing something in accordance with a definite plan. Since the mind naturally aligns to structure (like a step-by-step process), the SIT method feels familiar and therefore safe. The way out is through the same door we entered (the mind). For us to feel centered, we must first intellectually face and understand our pain. The SIT shows us how to do that.

The SIT method is a step process, but as we move through this sharing, you'll come to see how the SIT method is more a state of mind and a way of life than an actual step process. This entire book acts like a drip, and when mainlined into our system, can help us to be less ignorant in our beliefs and therefore take action to see the hurt and pain surrounding them. Even though I'll be sharing the SIT method with you in chapter 3, some of you may find you don't need to move through the steps because, after reading each chapter, you'll have seen yourself in a way you can't unsee yourself. This, for some, will lead to a lifestyle change that will no longer place blame on those around them because they will have discovered self-acceptance and self-awareness within. The choice in what you learn will be yours. For me, the more I SIT, the more centered I feel on all levels. I accept ALL of myself in that moment, therefore I no longer feel emotionally or physically broken.

Many people today feel the same way I did (overwhelmed and exhausted by their mental chatter) and are willing to find a dedicated path to feeling better, which is what discovering our center is all about.

I was taught during my first yoga instructor training that to find happiness meant balance must be found in all areas of life. This can include things like food, relationships, sex, and finances. For a long time, I bought into this mindset even though all it did was make me feel more out of control. For example, if I couldn't find balance in my diet, I felt worse about myself. Shame, guilt, frustration, and disappointment would filter in, and I'd end up trying to overeat those feelings.

In a way, it felt like it helped cushion my anxiety, but in reality, it was just another way of covering up the hurt within me. Masking my feelings kept what I couldn't stand about myself hidden, which gave it more power to control me the next time I felt the urge to eat my feelings away.

This, like my insecurity, became a behaviour that I couldn't stand feeling anymore. The only difference was that I didn't do anything about my over-eating until several years later (well into my 40s and is something I'll share more about later).

When I think of the word balance, I feel unsteady, like I'm walking on a tight rope with a pole in my hands. One side is going up and the other is going down as I attempt to establish balance. This is what was happening with my diet and eating habits. I wobbled back and forth from one extreme to the other. Whereas when I think of the word centred, I feel steady and grounded, and there's no wobble. To see a picture of what I mean, imagine a camera that's mounted to a gimble (you being the camera and the gimble representing life). No matter how much life shakes, you remain steady.

When I'm centred, my environment looks and feels stable and smooth as opposed to when I'm trying to find balance. However, feeling centered is not something we say to ourselves and then poof we're centered. Rather, it's an embodiment that happens when we see our way through a negatively charged belief. For us to truly grasp the meaning behind anything, we must go beyond the intellectual level to the core of our being (our feelings). To do this requires experience. As you read this book you may feel triggered. If you do, I encourage you to reflect upon your own experiences and feelings and examine some of your own hidden programs related to those triggering thoughts and feelings. I ask that you remain cognizant to any resistances brewing within you so that you may come to see and ultimately know yourself better.

If you feel called to, it might be helpful to keep a journal as you read and take notes to track your own progress.

Emotionally Off Center

Growing up with a mother who came from a traumatic and painful past was difficult. She chose to project this past onto those around her, even if she may not have been aware she was doing so. During childhood, I was often called a "stupid fucking retard" or a "dumb fucking cunt." It happened so often it became normal. That normal stored itself in my memory stick and became my familiar.

The same would apply to someone who grew up with a parent who told them they were intelligent. The only thing that determined whether one remark was positive or negative was perception. One person's point of view may be that the negative comment could have a positive spin and become a driving force toward success. From another perspective, it could have the opposite effect and be an impediment, which is what happened to me. The same is true of the positively conditioned comments.

Up until my 30s, I felt emotionally off-center. I rarely felt calm and relaxed and often felt anxious and insecure. This negatively impacted most of my relationships. It wasn't until I met my husband Chris that I felt motivated to change my state of mind. Chris and I got together right around the same time we both started instructing yoga. No matter how much Chris told me he loved me and went out of his way to prove it to me, I still felt deeply insecure about him being around other women. But rather than allowing it to ruin our relationship, I decided to do something about it.

My desire to be less anxious and insecure inspired me to travel to several different countries and try various modalities such as past life regression, accelerated meditation, body electronics, and breathwork training, just to name a few.

I'm not going to go into all the details of how body electronics work but I do want to mention how I reaped more benefits from it than I did from any other modality. To find out more information regarding body electronics, read Douglas W. Morrisons book titled _How We Heal_.

None of these modalities cured my emotional pain, but they were all necessary precursors to the next stage of my journey. Each one unveiled something hidden in me, some pleasant and some not pleasant. Back then I didn't know what I know today (my SIT method). That came several years later with experiences at home.

The Whiteout

Initially, when I'd arrive home from a trip, I'd feel better. However, that had more to do with the fact that I'd been away from my regular work schedule than anything else. I mention this only because if I had fully transformed something unwanted in me into something wanted, I would have felt the same whether I was traveling or at home. It's one of the reasons I've never felt confident about hosting any kind of health-related retreat out of town where the students couldn't go home each night. I want to make sure they aren't running away from their home life to get better.

I'm now going to share a story of one of my resistances to being in a group dynamic so you have a clearer idea of how guarded I was.

One of the first stops on my emotional healing expedition was at the Monroe Institute (Hemi-Sync headquarters and what I refer to as *accelerated meditation*, which is a form of meditation that from my perspective, uses binaural beats to manipulate brain wave oscillations). I learned a great deal while there but what was most significant for me was learning how to be comfortable around others.

You may be wondering how I could have instructed yoga classes full of people if I felt uncomfortable in groups, but the difference was I never had to interact with the yoga participants the way I did with the people in these retreats. The yoga participants in my class were not with me from morning till night.

Being in close quarters with strangers, sharing stories, and being vulnerable together would have driven me nuts if it hadn't been for one of the group participants named Betty. If a Monroe program wasn't fully booked, some people were assigned rooms to themselves, whereas if the program were booked, they would have to share. Since there were some spaces still available during this particular program, I was given my own room, which I was thrilled about.

I was in my room putting away my things when Betty came in to tell me she was going to be my roommate. She looked like Mrs. Claus and was the sweetest little old lady I'd ever seen.

"Hello, my name is Betty. I'm going to be your roommate. Do you mind if I take this bed?" she asked politely.

"Yes, I do mind. And no, you're not my roommate. This room has been assigned to me and only me. You'll have to go elsewhere to find your room," I snapped, glaring daggers at her.

"Oh, I see. But I'd really like to stay in this room if I could. The room I was assigned not only smells bad, but it also feels cold. So, if you don't mind, I'll stay here with you."

"But I do mind. So no," I piped back.

"Oh, I see," she said, her face falling. Putting her head down, she turned to walk out of the room, pulling her suitcase behind her like it weighed 100 pounds.

"Don't go!" The words startled even me. "I'm sorry for being rude. You can stay. Please come back."

I had a hard exterior but a soft inside. Throughout the first week of the program, I was short with all the participants. In my heart I never wanted to come off as standoffish and rude, but I couldn't help it. Being defensive was all I knew. It was my safe place. My reaction was a reflex that seemed to control me. Even when my heart said, "come close to me," my reflex said, "get away." For as long as I could remember, I felt guarded.

Within minutes of Betty putting her clothes away in our room, she had me keeled over laughing my head off. She turned out to be one of the funniest people I had ever met. The two of us became friends fast, and our almost constant and uncontrollable laughter either became infectious to those around us or annoying.

There was nearly a 40-year age gap between us, but when you're having fun and engulfed in the moment, age becomes irrelevant. Betty was the first to help open me up to the desire to want to feel connected with myself, and therefore, be close to others and as the years passed by, I couldn't help but become one of those people I couldn't stand in the past.

After completing several programs, learning how to be in a group dynamic helped me discover a plethora of things about myself. But the thing that stood out the most to me was how not wanting to connect with anyone was a reflection of me not wanting to connect with myself. I began to see how my lack of inner connection stemmed from a fear of being rejected. If I opened myself up and got rejected, it would trigger something I spent my whole life trying not to feel—that I was the lowest piece of scum on the earth.

Discovering these hidden things may seem small and insignificant to some, but to me, they were monumental. They opened the door to so many other discoveries within myself, including becoming comfortable enough to share my thoughts as I have in this book.

Chapter 2

BEING THE VICTIM

When beliefs are hidden, they have power to control us. This, in turn, makes us feel out of control, which can make us want to control others, and situations. Since we already feel powerless to the negative programs operating us, we remain frozen in a perpetual state of struggle. For those like myself this can lead to anxiety, depression, and physical exhaustion. Over time, when mental blockages like these are not addressed and repaired, they might even lead to terminal illness.

What's important to point out here is what we resist persists when we haven't unconditionally accepted how we feel. The more we remain asleep to that which has caused trauma, the more the pain overrides and controls us. But when we go straight into our hurt today and fully feel it without conditions or judgments, we deactivate the negative charge from our past, which sets us free from the need to control.

When we're asleep to our negative programs, we can't sense anything but war. However, when we genuinely want a better way of life, the information goes out into the world and our calls are answered by those on the same wavelength, like how this book came to you.

The more we see our way through our daily stresses, the more internally and externally connected we are. We begin to feel emotionally and physically lighter and brighter, and that opens the door to a deeper understanding of ourselves and of one another. This leads to less blame and more support.

For example, what I'm sharing here is not me teaching you something you don't already know. We are vibrationally lining up with one another, and in doing so, I'm reminding you of what you might have forgotten while caught in the filtered lens of your pain. I'm you in the sense that I am an embodiment of ALL information, just as you are to me. We are one another's conduits to hear ourselves.

We wake ourselves up through one another, and when we realize this, not only do we organize internal and external chaos, (meaning that when we quiet our mental chatter, outer noise becomes quiet) but we also set ourselves free from the bondage of ranking ourselves and others. I no longer see others as my teacher or guru or vice versa. No one is standing above one another. We are equals standing together on the same platform—all partitions crumble. This does not mean that we stop teaching one another things and should stop learning for ourselves. When we doubt but still have a desire to know, the so-called teacher appears. When we trust, we become the teacher passing information onto others. In this sense, we all are teachers and students, learning from each other and passing that information on. But no one is bigger or smaller.

Loving Yourself

Initially when I began to seek out a way to heal my mental pain, I thought I was doing it for Chris so I didn't lose him. But as time passed, I began to realize that I was doing it for myself. I didn't want to lose the person I knew I could become (a confident and self-assured person) because of an insecure program from the past. Throughout my travels abroad and during my internal travels at home, I realized Chris was my placebo to feeling better. Wanting to heal my pain for Chris led me to me. When I understood this, I also understood that if I'd been wanting to feel better solely for Chris, I would have still been holding him responsible for my happiness. I would have been in the same selfish relationship I'd been in my whole life—a relationship with the ignorant side of myself that said, "make me happy so I can be happy."

When I returned home from my travels, I bought myself a wedding ring. I moved Chris's ring over to my pinky finger—not to discredit our marriage or my love for Chris, but because my wedding ring was and still is a symbol of my commitment and marriage to myself. Because I married someone that genuinely loved me, Chris understood and supported my decision.

I felt that wearing Chris's ring on my wedding finger symbolized that I was putting Chris before me, and that Chris had some sort of ownership over me. After four years of traveling to heal my fragmented mind (something I am continually working on today), I realized I did it all for myself. Therefore, I was first. I also realized that Chris didn't love me because he wanted to capture me. Chris fell in love with me because of the freedom he felt inside of himself when he was with me. That is how love is meant to be—unchartered, unharnessed, unbound, free, and therefore unconditional.

The moment I feel a desire to blame or justify something is the same moment I know I've lost my mind. Today, I no longer need Chris or anyone else to complete me, and when I do I SIT. *Seeing it Through* reroutes and reminds me to love myself in a way that no one else could ever come close to. When I truly love myself and don't ask this of others, I give freedom to those around me. That, to me, is what real love is.

Having a loving relationship with one another is easier when we have a loving relationship with ourselves. Even so, like all relationships, there are always things to work on, and when we are willing, can help us to see ourselves in a better light.

The Victim Mindset

I traveled far and wide to experience many different healing modalities because a part of me knew I would undergo a mental peeling that would expose my own inner knowledge. This made me feel raw and exposed, which dredged up deeper layers of anger and resentment towards my mother, making me feel like a victim.

Every day I felt trapped inside my head. The insecurity I felt surrounding my relationship with Chris seemed to be rerouted and replaced with anger towards my mother. I didn't realize just how much hurt from my childhood I had tucked away until it was there, and I was unable to get away from it. At the time, I couldn't understand why the actions I took to feel better made me feel worse. It felt like all the self-work I'd done was now punching me in the face. All I could think about was how my mother ruined my life, and that it was her bad parenting that prevented me from being confident and successful.

Since our emotions tune our environments, that's exactly what I got back. Being in defense mode also put me in attack mode in much the same way a porcupine's quills go up when he's defending himself. Wallowing in my past attracted situations for me to feel more victimized. For example, some years ago one of the studio owners I worked for (I'll call her Shirley) asked me to come in on my day off to get acupuncture from her friend visiting from China.

"It's a great deal, only $40 per session for my instructors and students," she said.

Even though my initial gut reaction said, "no don't go," I went anyway because I wanted approval from Shirley. This was a by-product of the belief that I hadn't received approval from my mother.

When I arrived for the session, Shirley prepped me by saying, "Oh and don't be a baby Jennifer, my friend is not like North American acupuncturist's. He's a real acupuncturist and uses thicker needles than what you might have been used to."

Her comment didn't force me to do anything, but it did trigger me to have an emotional response that encouraged me to want to keep quiet rather than protect myself. I later realized during one of my SITs this was an outgrowth of an early childhood belief that if I was good and quiet enough my mom would want to pick me up, hold me, and love me.

To make a long story short, both my lungs were punctured during the acupuncture session. The doctor called it a double pneumothorax, but that wasn't what made me feel like a victim. Instead, it was Shirley's response. When I called her to tell her what happened, she told me that I must be mistaken since no one else she knew complained of anything like that happening to them.

I didn't realize it at the time, but her response triggered the story that my mom didn't want to take any responsibility for ruining my life. This of course only made me angrier and more resentful toward Shirley. The pent-up frustration and resentment I felt toward Shirley became another log on top of the already raging fire I felt towards my mother.

Like many things that initially seem negative, this experience had a silver lining. It ended a year long silence between my mother and me. Five minutes after I drove away from the x-ray clinic, I got a call from the technician informing me of the results. In a panic on my way to the hospital, I called my mom to tell her what happened. This is what opened the door and allowed us to begin to mend our broken relationship.

On an energetic level, the feelings I'd harboured toward my mother needed a place to go. I believe my inability to grieve the hurt I felt as a child was stored in my lungs. That may not be the case for everyone, but our bodies hold our emotions somewhere.

Whatever the emotion, as time went on and I did nothing to *See It Through*, the suppressed feelings mounted. In time they found a way to let the pressure out (in this case it was the acupuncture incident, which was essentially my emotional field working in conjunction with my employer and her acupuncturists friends' field). This was an experience that had to surface and was a way for my body to show me what my emotional pain felt like on a physical level. The hurt I felt was deeply wired in my brain and actively firing. This meant that my brain's filter system was doing its job and was seeking out ways to confirm my unresolved pain.

Even though soon afterward I understood, energetically, how and why the acupuncture incident took place, I still didn't process it in a way that made me feel free. That didn't happen until SIT 2 arrived. Yes, the door was open between me and my mom, but because I denied accepting how I really felt, I ended up attracting more situations that caused me to feel victimized.

Having said that, in reality there's no such thing as a bully or a victim—there's only emotional fields colliding. We label ourselves the victim or bully by denying unconditional acceptance of our emotions.

Later, after I rewrote my childhood a few times, I was able to realize that the more I refused to feel the hurt from my mom the more I attracted hurt women to hurt me. When we believe beyond a reasonable doubt that the label (victim, for example) is who we are, it becomes our identity. The victim, like all other identities, looks for excuses that will justify its position, saying things like "These feelings are not mine—they were passed down to me, therefore I don't have to take responsibility for them." This gives the victim an excuse to remain relevant, while keeping its host asleep and rendering them to feel more like a victim.

Releasing Your Burden

I have found for me that the more I SIT, the less burdened I am. The more layers I see my way through, the more light fills in to replace the old conditioning. Human life is a constant peeling. That's why no matter how many messes we clean up, there's always more. The more we SIT, the less hard our lives feel. So, even though the messes may come up, they don't burden us like they used to.

It's my belief that we are here in these physical bodies to evolve. Our Souls didn't come here to kick back in the pool and drink margarita's all day—we came here to mature. Therefore, our Souls want to be challenged. Challenge creates purpose. For some of you, reading this book is going to be a challenge because it will force you to look at your ignorance.

When I'm not in denial and blaming my outer reality for how I'm feeling, I have limitless life coursing through my veins. If I need someone else to make me happy, I'll never be mentally or physically well because I'm suffering over someone saving me. I'll continue to find people to confirm my neediness in different ways and hold them responsible for it. When they can't, I'll blame them for it. The SIT method shows us how to see and use our stressful situations with others as a way to evolve. Instead of running away from our struggles, we run straight into and through them.

It's important to get in touch with your feelings so that you can learn to trust who you are. That way you're no longer attached to needing someone else's approval to make you feel complete. This will allow you to replace old conditioning with new understandings, which can help to establish inner trust. This can also become a source of inspiration to ourselves and to those around us, and when we no longer need other people to tell us who we are we won't need them to fill our emotional voids.

When we go inwards and reflect, we allow others to live their lives—meaning we don't feel the need to control them to make ourselves feel better.

Rewriting Your Childhood

In closing this chapter, I am going to leave you with something that helped me begin mending the relationship with my mom.

Rewrite your childhood to change your timeline.

When you rewrite your childhood, you rewrite new beliefs into the present. This can provide a different landscape to experience and expand upon. The idea of rewriting my childhood came to me first, followed by letting all sounds in (something we will soon discover), and the SIT methods. Rewriting your childhood is an excellent precursor to a SIT.

I found that when I rewrote my past, which for years I believed lacked love, I erased doubt. In its place, I discovered an abundance of love. When I feel trust, which is opposite of doubt, I remember the good times from my childhood. This has allowed me to feel my mother's love for me today, even when her words and actions say something different. Rewriting my childhood came as a pleasant surprise, as the more I dug for things I wasn't fixated on, the less resentful I felt. But don't take my word for it—see how it resonates for you.

For the most part, people live their lives unaware that they do so from a place in the past. This influences the decisions they make in their adult lives. We may have told ourselves that our past is over and that it doesn't bother us. But if we haven't come to terms with it, our hopes and dreams will be crushed. We will carry the past with us. Others will pick it up and then throw it back at us.

If we feel victimized in life today, if things are not going the way we want them to, and we feel beaten up, it's likely because of the way we wrote our past in our minds. Focusing on a negative past brings on more negativity today. If we don't land the job, get the relationship we desire, achieve the ideal body weight, or move to the perfect city, it's because our past is writing over the top of where we are today. We must change our perception of the past in order to adjust the way we live our lives in the present.

Our beliefs place us on automatic pilot, and that can be both a negative and a positive—meaning we can instill both negative and positive programming. This exercise is geared towards remembering the good times we had, not to deflect from the so-called bad but instead as a way to broaden and expand our perception of today. Remember more good times from the past and you won't feel like you're being pulled backwards in the present. When we are fixated only on the bad, we're not emotionally (and thus vibrationally) open to seeing the positive today.

This aligns us to unfulfilling jobs and relationships. What we focus our attention on our brain downloads and then finds. For example, if you had a lack of money growing up and it's what you remember most, you'll see lack in most if not all places you look today—even if you have millions of dollars. When our thinking is not in receiving mode, we're unable to regularly align with people, places, and situations that may be of great assistance to us. In a roundabout way, we'll learn a bit later on how when we combine both sides of the battery (positive and negative), we can still react to life while remaining open to overflowing wellness. Rewriting your childhood is not about deflecting—it's about reflecting more on the things we made less relevant, and then as a by-product, became hidden.

Focus on bringing forgotten memories into the light to positively influence our footprint today. Start by asking, "Where did I feel good?" If your mind automatically goes to where you didn't, ask the question repeatedly until your brain finds an answer. For some, feeling good could have come from your memories of walking to or being at school. For others, it might be playing with an animal, riding your bike, spending time with friends, or being on your own. If too much time on your own feels negative, ask yourself if there was anything you liked about being alone. Just remember it's important not to push yourself to like something, as it will only create more tension. Also, keep in mind that you're asking to see if there's an opening there. A tip when asking is to sit with your eyes closed. Take a few breaths in and out while relaxing your body first. If your already tense asking the question, you might want to skip right past the question without giving the part of yourself that believes there is an opening a fair chance to respond. If there is an opening, even a small one, focus on it by breathing and relaxing into the memory, giving it room to expand. Giving one good memory life may give another life. If not, move on to another area of your life. The goal during this exercise is to uncover and rediscover times you enjoyed or felt peaceful or loved. Remembering one good memory cracks the closed door open. When this happens, we feel less confined and have more breathing room. Our perception widens and with it, we feel less limited. This enables us to begin seeing more opportunities. Paving the way for us to later, be more willing to use the negative to our advantage and combine both sides of the battery.

When I rewrote my childhood, I did it because I wanted to feel better. I also didn't want to hold the weight of resentment towards my mother anymore. Most days I would think about how she ruined my life or all the bad things she said and did that led me to believe she was the cause of all my problems. So, instead of holding onto the same old victimized story in my head, I put pen to paper and encouraged myself to seek out the good memories and write them down.

For me, it's important to write the memories down so that my mind doesn't try to forget or argue with it later. Rewriting your childhood simply involves you sitting down with a pad and pen, silencing your mind and body, and doing your best to seek out memories that make you feel better than those you already have stockpiled and filed away.

Stay true to the facts. Collecting the proof from good memories and thoughts is not something that can be faked—your mind needs to believe that these things really did happen. Faking is lying, which bolsters doubt instead of trust. Therefore, faking can cause us to feel more grief later.

Many of us, myself included, will have to dig deep to find even one positive memory. This will often trigger the release of another, and then another after that. I found that a second or a third surfaced in mere days, or sometimes weeks following the first. In this case, make sure you go back and add these memories to your list. Finding one good memory is going to be a starting point, which is all you need to get the engine started.

This is also something you can do if you believe you had a traumatic womb or birth experience. When I began having flashbacks of being in the womb at age 33, I'd feel instant panic and terror. During this time, I asked my mom if she was going through anything while pregnant with me. She said my dad was out with other women allot and probably cheating on her. She also said she didn't want to have me. Both these stresses along with her already painful past, gave her anxiety to the point where she underwent daily panic attacks from it. Since it is my belief that while in the womb, we download our mothers' feelings, her sharing this information, validated my flashbacks.

When I began rewriting my time in the womb, I began uncovering memories I didn't know were there—memories that made me feel less claustrophobic and alone. Without going into too much detail, I recall there being other loving states of consciousness that were there with me then that are still with me today.

From the moment I began writing about the good memories, the disjointed feelings within me began to heal. From there, more extraordinary incidents began to occur in my personal and professional life. I didn't realize the weight I carried until it was gone.

We all have something from our past that blocks our view of today. Until we rewrite it into a new, authentic perspective, we will never be free, mentally or physically, in our today.

Chapter 3

SIT METHOD PART ONE

I am calling this SIT 1 not because it should come first before SIT 2, but because this was the order it came about. I found for me, rewriting your childhood was essential to do before SIT 1 because of how I viewed my childhood.

The first part of SIT 1 not only helps us to become aware of how we are feeling (emotions), but it also makes us aware of other time zones from our past and present that impact our future. This is important because when we understand how time works, it doesn't have the same power it once did. When we realize we are the ones in control of time, we feel less threatened by it.

You may decide after reading both SIT methods that part one is your method of choice. If so, great. It's important that you don't push yourself into something you don't feel ready to do or that doesn't resonate with you. I mention this because as we will come to discover, since part two of the SIT method is based around exploring and diving fully into emotions, it may not be everyone's cup of tea. All these methods combined have been what has worked and continues to work for me.

There was a year gap between the SIT methods, and I believe that happened on purpose. For me to be able to emotionally digest part two, I needed a full year with part one first. There are days where when I'm not feeling up for the challenge that SIT 2 can sometimes bring (due to the level of emotional intensity that can come from it), and so I'll go with SIT 1 instead. I have found both SIT methods decrease mental suffering for me.

At the start of the book, I asked that you pay attention to how you feel as you're reading any piece of literature. Notice what stirs in you on an emotional level. Allow your gut instinct to lead you rather than overthinking it in your head, as the head tends to energetically wonder off from the physical body, rendering some of us feeling less grounded and more anxious.

When we SIT, we time travel. We do this by understanding that when we bring a negatively charged belief from our past into our now, we make the now toxic. We come to see that the past is not something behind us, rather it lives inside of us.

When we believe that we are tied to an event, a part of us remains there. Our brain stores the data of the event and later uses this information as a reference point to help us decide how we live our lives today. I use the word help because as you will soon come to know, life is always assisting us, even when we think it's not. For example, what we emotionally activate most, our environment will arrange and provide for us. This is why many of us don't see life as happening *for* us and instead feel victimized by it happening *to* us. One of the many things this book does is it helps us expose our negative conditioning so that we don't feel like we're being held prisoners to it.

When we SIT, we're not going back to the past to grovel and get stuck in something—we're seeking to get through to the other side of the struggle. When we try to get over something, we stay broken. But if we move through it, emotionally to accept and release it, we can be transformed into another state of being.

I no longer go out of my way to cast off things that bother me. I don't pretend they don't bother me when they do or try to positive talk my way out. Exposing negative programming can be life changing when we welcome it into our lives. Running only makes us exhausted. When we SIT, we remember who we are and are no longer running from something that scares us. When we SIT, we purposely see that which is hidden in us so that it no longer effects or controls us.

Often when wanting to heal ourselves, we think it first must come with forgiving someone. What is forgiveness? When the word is spoken from a place of unresolved hurt, it can leave us feeling more pent-up. We feel as though we must forgive the other person to live a peaceful life. This is simply not the truth. Forgiveness happens when we see our way through the negative charge, unconditionally accepting how we really feel. Anything outside of that survives in a figment of our imagination from the past that we bring with us into our today.

Healing Broken Thinking

I held a grudge against my mother until my late 30s while repeatedly telling myself I had to forgive her. I couldn't, at the time, let go of the thinking mind that said I must forgive her to be free. But when I was able to see behind the scenes of the reels that spilled out of me, forgiving my mother no longer mattered to me. We do not have to forgive the person we feel threatened by, nor do we have to like them. When we *See It Through,* we're no longer being controlled by the negative charge surrounding the story, so we don't feel the same way anymore. Therefore, not only do we set ourselves free from holding onto unnecessary emotional weight, but we also set the other person free. This is essentially what forgiveness is to me.

To heal broken thinking, and possibly a broken body as well, it's necessary that we see our way through any and every prickly point of confusion in us. To alchemize pain into joy, we must first understand the pain, which cannot be meditated or breathed away. This is something that we must face head on with our minds. For the familiar in us to be transformed into non-familiar, the mind needs to feel supported. It's important to establish an intellectual platform, a procedure or step-process that will help guide it to its destination. There must first be a path that makes logical sense. When we SIT, we use our smarts to punch a hole in the boxed mind so that combined light filters outward (light comes from within then projects out).

There are many existing self-help methods that could be considered SIT methods but aren't referred to as such because the name was born out of my consciousness. A couple examples of SIT methods are Byron Katie's *The Work* or Colin Tipping's *Radical Forgiveness*. Many SIT methods come with different techniques but will have one thing in common: to help us see our way through struggle. There are many current methods. Choosing the right method for you is your decision.

Seeing it Through allows the mind to reveal new and improved ways of seeing its mathematical self. It shines a spotlight on all our lies, doubts, and insecurities. It allows us to understand we can, and do, affect our past from within today. We are the ones that make time happen simultaneously whenever we choose to do so or not. The past cannot hurt us when we understand that we are in control of it. It is not a dead zone that we can never again get to. Rather it's alive and well each time we think it into our today. If our past is toxic and we bring it forward to the present, we will make today toxic as well. The choice is always ours, and we alone can decide what kind of day we desire. No one else decides that for us. The sooner we realize this, the sooner we can change the course of our timeline!

Cognitive Dissonance

The intellectual knows only what is in front of it since that's what it has been taught to do. The more educated, the harder it can be to convince someone of something they are unfamiliar with. This is called cognitive dissonance and occurs when we've been taught something for so long that when taught the opposite, our brain cannot immediately accept it. We feel defensive when what we believe to be true is challenged and defend the boxed-in viewpoint. When the mind is willing to embark upon a self-educated journey, the SIT method works. The programmed mind thrives on proof, which is what the SIT encourages. So, let's use it to our advantage! Use an educated mind to navigate our thinking mind into a knowing mind that trusts itself. This is how we *break bottom* and embody the real top to get to ground zero and the Soul Center (below floor 1), something I'll explain more in chapter 8.

The more you *See It Through*, the less negatively charged beliefs stick to you. A belief sticks to you only because it's drawn to what is already in you. When you deactivate the negative charge surrounding the feeling, your brain's filter system, which is a group of neurons in your brain called the RAS (reticular activating system), aligns you to positive or neutral situations. When you learn something new, the reticular activating system's job is to help you see and hear it everywhere.

For example, if you learn from a young age that life is meant to be a struggle and do nothing to change that belief, RAS will look for ways to prove that back to you from your environment via people, places, and situations. Your brain only does its job, and it is of great importance that you do not criticize it for doing so. Apply yourself to feeling better and your brain will help turn that into a reality.

SIT 1

Before I share the SIT process, let me first say you cannot pretend your way into a belief. To change a view, you must collect data to convince yourself of the truth. Faking your way inevitably takes you further from your lighthouse. It also moves you further from the solution. When you fake an emotion or a belief, more lies are serving you. Because of this, you must learn to be honest with yourself.

Know that beliefs do not hypnotize us—we hypnotize ourselves into beliefs by not trusting. This SIT method is designed to help us snap out of being hypnotized over our stressful stories. When we are stuck in our stories, we're not energetically in our physical body.

Therefore, we are stuck in our head in a power outage. If willing, the SIT method will allow us to consciously program new beliefs into existence so that when these reels spin, they don't knock us out as the negative reels do. Instead, they will help keep us awake even when our eyes are closed so that we are no longer being controlled by old negative reels.

Here's a guide for how to get started with this practice:

1. *Write your issue in one sentence only.* If you give that negative thought an inch, it'll take a mile.
2. *Write down the emotion you are feeling over the issue.* One word only.
3. *Say out loud: "Right now in this moment, I believe that I "am ..."* (the emotion)." *Followed by: "Right now in this moment I am being run by the program called* "anger." I am placing *emphasis* on *this* moment so that you are aware of your current time zone. Also, it's important that you say this out loud, as now the program has been spotted and is now no longer hiding. It already has less control over you.

4. *Notice the time zone you're looking at.* Become conscious that there are now two time zones in effect. You have the image, or roughly the age, from your past and you have where you are right now. Close your eyes and see this distinction. Now open your eyes and see where you are in this moment. See how you have just brought both time zones together in the same room. Recognize that you are in control of your past. You are taking a moment to see how time is linear and how it behaves according to your decision making.

5. *Write down the belief that is opposite from question number two.* Follow this by writing down everywhere in your life that you see this opposite. When you have finished your list, read it over at least one more time today. Then read it again when the emotion resurfaces. I used the word *when* and not *if* because to tell yourself that you will never experience the emotion again would be absurd. What we are doing in this step is clearing the chaos in the belief that covers one story, not all of them. The more you practice this, the less power the beliefs will have over you the next time they surface.

6. *Go to the past image you have brought forward today and remind yourself that you are the one in control of your timeline. Repeat this out loud*: "I can clearly see that you (the image or feeling of your past self) are here with me right now in one body. You are not behind me. You are here inside me and with me always. When I feel well today, you automatically feel well today. Where I go, you go. I can change where we were in the past because I know that my point of power is now in this moment. The past is not in control of me. I am in control of it, which is how I can bridge the gap between you and me becoming we. Together we are now "I." You are no longer apart from me, and if there comes a day when I think that you are, I will remember my way back to you and bridge that gap.

7. *SMILE* as you are telling your other self this and see them smile back at you. Your past self in this moment is not somewhere else suffering. They are here with you. When you are suffering today, it is only ever because you have forgotten where your point of power is.

This step process first came to me after one of the many times my mom told me to go fuck myself and hung up on me. My body was flooded with adrenaline. I felt like I had no blood in my limbs. I was triggered to feel abandonment, resentment, anger, and even rage—all of which had me feeling sick to my stomach.

For example, after she hung up on me, I left my house and went for a walk. The emotions I was feeling were all too consuming to sit still with. I needed to physically move. Around 10 minutes of stewing in anger on my walk I had an epiphany. The thought "since I feel consumed in anger, I must also believe that I am anger" led me to say out loud, "In this moment I believe I am anger. Since I believe I am anger right now, I can also see how in this moment I am being operated by an anger program." Seeing this made me feel more human and the program more inhuman (AI). I immediately sensed the program anger as being something outside of me. Something I was unknowingly choosing to install and ingest into my system that would ultimately give me emotional and sometimes even physical indigestion. Therefore, it is valuable for us to take advantage of being triggered. IT exposes programming. The more we uncover, the less charged, reactive, and unwell we feel.

As I walked and the words flowed out of me, I realized that when I feel consumed by an emotion it's because I've gone semiconscious to the emotion. For the most part, it's all I can sense. The emotion has the majority of power. I'm not thinking my way into anger, instead I'm reacting to it.

I could tell the anger was buried deep within me and I wanted to know where it was coming from. Thinking about this and asking myself this question also made me aware that there were two time zones happening at once. That reminded me of my point of power and how it resides in this time zone, not the one I was imagining. Knowing where my point of power is allowed me to be able to positively influence my past, changing how I felt in the present.

Rather than allowing my mind to race to several different places, I focussed my attention on the first stop. The first thing, no matter how insignificant it may initially appear, is the most relevant. When I look back now almost two years later, I no longer remember the memory—and that's a good thing, because it proves to me that I have moved through it and I'm no longer attached and controlled by it the way I was before. This is something that happens when we see our way through that which pains us. It's not that we forget the memory, although that can happen. When we allow ourselves to remember and experience the feelings from our past, we deactivate the negative charge surrounding the memory and make the memory less painful (or even pain free). All pain is brought on by a desire not to feel, something we will discover in a later chapter.

Overcoming Doubt with SIT

Let me share one of my SIT experiences regarding doubt. It came in like a hurricane one afternoon, hitting me so hard I felt sick to my stomach. Moving through doubt that day took a lot of discipline. I am always amazed by how overwhelming a belief can feel in the moment that it spirals.

A friend called to tell me about her new career success. At that time, I didn't consider myself to be a good friend to her. She usually instigated most of our interactions. Her news flooded my stomach, creating a massive pit of dread. What am I doing with my life? Where am I going? When am I ever going to make something of myself? Everyone is successful except me.

I am stupid and unsuccessful. In that moment, I made her achievement all about me and was unable to share her happiness because I was too busy being operated.

SIT 1 was born a few days earlier when I worked through the program anger that was triggered from my mother hanging up on me. I believe this session is what helped me quickly and almost effortlessly break away from making her news all about me. Normally, I would have let the reckless feelings consume me throughout the day and carried their weight on my shoulders.

After our conversation, like when my mother hung up on me, I needed to move my body, so I took the dogs for a walk. There are times I need to get out of my surroundings and move the unsettling emotional brew as it bubbles up and other times where I feel like sitting physically still. Because I am familiar with the SIT, I am comfortable not writing it down while walking and instead work through it in my head. Just keep in mind it's important in the beginning to write your thoughts on paper when you get home so that your mind doesn't try to argue with it later.

As I walked my mind filled with doubt, but it enabled the question to rise. *What am I believing about myself right now? I believe that I am doubt, but where did this doubt come from?* As the words parted my lips an image popped up. (Yes, I was speaking aloud, which is important, as it makes the words less powerful. When words are confined to our head, they fill up the space making us feel cramped, and small while they get bigger. Letting the words out is like letting hot air out of a balloon or taking the lid off a boiling pot.) I saw myself standing in the back entrance of the house I grew up. As usual, I was late for my tenth-grade class. I stood, feeling lost, confused, and most importantly, unsupported—not only by my parents but by me, the most significant person. *What am I going to do with my life? I'm going nowhere, and I'm terrified.*

I continued walking and understood how all these past thoughts flooded into where I was in that moment. One image slid over another, bringing with them a past time zone to eclipse the present.

I felt the strong allure of past beliefs, but I pushed myself forward to apply action to accountability. This is the moment so many of us turn and run. *Jennifer, you are going to snap yourself out of this trance right flipping now! I know where my point of power is—here in this moment where my physical feet stand—not back in the images from the past.*

Speaking the words "snap out of it" helps me back into my body so that I can be in the present where I can think more clearly.

What don't you doubt about yourself? I don't doubt my work with clients nor my yoga facilitation – they are my center of confidence. With the word *confidence*, the heaviness began to lift, and my mind immediately sought out the areas in my life where I felt unquestioningly confident. It ranks with trust and reminds me of all the points where I can see and feel confidence and verify them as places where I trust myself.

My friend telling me about her success became about finding my own success in the moment. Jolting myself out of this memory of negatively charged beliefs helped me want to be happy for my friend. My point of power is always right here, now, and anything beyond that causes me pain.

When I first heard about my friend's newfound success, I shot straight out of my physical body only to mentally go in a hundred different directions toward a hundred different dead-ends, which is all there is when we're inside the box.

Feeling safe was the one thing I told myself I needed most while growing up but never believed I received. I felt unsafe, and doubting my status then was something I carried with me until that day. Doubt had blocked me from immediately being there for my friend.

That afternoon I watched doubt alchemize into trust just as I had watched anger days before transform into joy. The fact that I had the power to shatter all veils affected me in the most powerful way. I felt safe and in control, which made me let go of needing to be in control. *Now that's power.*

The more trust I felt in my life, the safer I felt about where I stood. The more I felt my point of power, the happier and more excited I felt for my friend. With that realization came the freedom to soar high. I understood that nothing feels better than being sincerely happy for another's success. Experiencing joy for someone else left me feeling extremely successful.

I tried to tell myself to be happy for her, but because I clearly wasn't feeling that way about myself, it only made me feel envious. I want to feel success for myself and for others every day of my life. It is of primary importance now for me to SIT in each obstacle that comes my way. If I don't, I allow the little things to pile on top of bigger things. When I'm triggered, they all crash down onto me.

Success in life is born out of feeling personally successful. To remain successful, we must address all uncomfortable emotions. Otherwise, we risk losing everything we worked so hard to accomplish.

When I stay dedicated to seeing my way through all negatively charged beliefs (NCB), good things happen. Following my walk, I received a message from an old friend I'd wanted to reconnect with for several years but never tried to because of doubt. She messaged me to say she missed me and that she would love to reconnect. Her message proved to me that when I connect to myself, others feel connected to me to.

We may find after having moved through several sessions of this or other SIT methods, we no longer use it in its entirety. Maybe on some days we leave out or add steps. The more accountable for action, the more aware we become.

This may lead us to creating our own SIT method. I shared my doubt experience to demonstrate why it is not necessary to follow each step. However, I also believe in the early stages, it can be highly beneficial to do so.

Chapter 4

THE TWO ATMOSPHERES AND OXYGEN

There are two sides to our thinking: the mind (trust) and the ghost (doubt). The combination is what creates purpose. The ghost makes us want to doubt ourselves and the mind makes us want to trust ourselves. Purpose happens when the ghost and mind unite. Ghost is the negative side of the battery and mind is the positive side. Just because ghost is negative doesn't make it bad. Think about it this way—without ghost we wouldn't feel motivated to want to change unhappiness. We see from this perspective, how ghost is an essential part of growth.

For example, if you were lying in a comfortable bed, how would you know it was comfortable without knowing what uncomfortable felt like? Ghost makes us feel uncomfortable in order to inspire us to want to get out there and improve our life.

The problem some of us have is we become fixated on the negative and lose sight of the destination. This is where mind comes in, acting like a barometer to help steer us back on track.

Repairing our thinking isn't solely about looking for the positive—it's about seeing how the two go together. This is how we accept ALL of ourselves, not just the positive parts. When we don't accept the negative, we give it power to operate and control us.

To be comfortable, both ends of the battery must connect to a circuit to create power. This, essentially, is what we're learning to do as we move through this read together. Discovering how to spot our negative behaviour (because it hides) before it takes us over is vital. In doing so, we can learn how to use it as a springboard to a better life.

Reality vs. Reelality

We fluctuate between two different atmospheres that contain two different energy bodies: reality (mind) and reelality (ghost). These atmospheres also contain two different qualities of air (something I'll mention more in the latter half of this chapter). The word *reelality* is not a typo, it's a word I have come up with to describe the movie state of mind many of us drift in and out of daily. When we doubt, we activate the ghost and when we trust we activate the mind.

We all have different beliefs running in us, like movie reels. In reelality, we are on autopilot to our DNA script. This is similar to when you watch a movie on TV or in the theatre and everything around you in reality falls away. In reelality, we become hypnotized by negatively charged movie clips that reel out of us. One negative thought attaches to another negative thought, and those thoughts contain images (reels) that hold and emit vibrations. A reel holds a collage of minute images in place, and when the wheel holding it rotates, the images merge into a reel-life motion picture.

Reels start out as single images put into motion by a person's interpretation of them. For example, an image of a couple holding hands might appear as a single image in one person's mind. To another who may be having relationship issues it may play out as an entire movie. When we are caught in a reel, we are caught in a thought pattern. If you don't have relationship issues, the thought about the couple holding hands floats by without a second thought attached to it.

When we give these reels momentum, they make a "reel" life motion picture for us to watch and become captivated by, then we project the movie over reality. Ever see that old commercial that's designed to remind people not to drink and drive during the Christmas holidays? The one that stockpiles one beer glass after another in front of the drivers face until after one too many, the driver is unable to see the road and ends up smashing into another car? That's what negatively charged beliefs do. They filter our view so we can't see reality. When we are caught in this kind of headspace, we're unable to see if it's a friendly universe. It's also how one negative thinker attracts other negative thinkers. Negatively charged beliefs collide with other lower frequencies like it.

When a thought rises and we are stressed by it—even if for a moment—it's because we have made it into a belief. Believing a stressful thought places a negative charge on it. Before a thought is made stressful, it's more like a cloud floating in the sky. We don't even notice it until we create a rainstorm that falls on us.

The moment a thought is made into an NCB (negatively-charged belief) is the same moment we move out of reality and into reelality. Now we're not only trying to survive a negative thought, but we're being operated by it. From the moment the belief becomes absolute, it runs you, gains control, and has all the power. For example, when my dog Abby passed, I'd wake up each morning the same way I'd go to bed each night—in total and complete terror. Panic attacks would come on and it felt like there was nothing I could do to stop them. They were in control of me. The belief that I was not going to survive without her put me in a power outage that gave the

NCB the power to consume and terrorize me. Reelality is the unfriendly, stress filled, anxiety ridden, paranoid, insecure, arrogant, ignorant, and fearful universe that makes us feel unsafe. It's a world I know very well, having had spent so much time there.

Reality, on the other hand, is the all-encompassing friendly universe—a world free from mental restraints. When we are in reality it's because we are in a peaceful and effortless state of mind. Therefore, we are in our physical bodies. Relaxed thinking is an open mind, which equals rest, digest, repair mode (parasympathetic nervous system). Whereas a closed mind (ghost) equals fight or flight mode (sympathetic nervous system). When our thinking is restless, we have a nervous-nervous system, and that kicks us mentally out of our physical body. Our thinking has gone astral like a ghost. When we *See It Through*, our mind relaxes, we digest the moment, and then our body mimics that.

I've explained it to the participants in my yoga classes this way: Our physical bodies cannot be in repair mode so long as we are not willing to embrace all feelings rising in that moment while in the pose. You could be practicing yoga, but if all you're doing while in one pose is trying to get to the next, you're bypassing the present moment.

More importantly, though, would be to ask yourself the question, "Why are you trying to get to the next pose? Is the current pose dredging up uncomfortable feelings you don't want to feel right now?" Until we are emotionally able to be *in* body, we will continue to look for ways to be out of it. Therefore, it won't matter how flexible and strong you appear to be on the outside. As long as your mentally removed, your body will be in fight or flight mode wearing you down. If we want our bodies to be in rest, digest, and repair mode (which is essentially the body healing itself), we must be energetically in our bodies and lovingly accept every feeling we experience. Having said that, it's important that we don't try to force ourselves to love everything that's coming up. When we do, we create further resistance, something I explain more later.

The Importance of Soul, Body, and Mind

What's important to point out here (because it sheds light on who's in control of the vehicle) is that whether we're relaxing our physical bodies or creating a lot of movement, we are doing it through our thinking first. The body doesn't move you—you move it. For example, ask yourself how you got to work this morning. Did your body drag you there, or was it your thinking? When ghost is in the driver's seat, it will lead us to believe that body is less evolved than essence (Soul). In reality, body is the physical counterpart of Soul. Therefore, it is just as evolved.

The body also holds and emanates our feelings, which, when fully embraced and felt by us, align us to reality. So, even though it is our thinking that initially determines how our bodies feel, when we don't treat our bodies as equal to Soul they feel discarded and, over time, become less receptive to our demands. Meaning, the less we feel, the denser the body will feel, and the harder it will be to find control. A lack of feeling equals a lack of self-acceptance, which also equals reelality, a lack of oxygen, and disease.

When we allow our minds to be still, the same theme plays into our daily lives. When we obsess over the image of seeing ourselves somewhere we are not (future self), we struggle because we believe happiness lives over there.

The mind is the Soul's form in reality. Therefore, mind makes matter. Ghost is the astral body that energetically leaves the physical body when a negative charge is present. When the mind doubts, its other personality, the ghost, takes over. This is why when ghost is active, we sometimes feel emotionally chaotic. Emotional chaos is exactly as it sounds. These are emotions without any rhyme or reason that are often confused, unfocused, and can change rapidly. You could be angry one second, laughing the next, and crying shortly after. You could feel a mixture of frustration and joy at the same time. This state of being feels hectic internally, and that same chaos spreads to your external interactions in daily life.

A closed mind feels like a box. It's the ghost's compressed and confined limited reality. Since the ghost's mindset is to overthink, all thinking is the box. If you can't get out of your head and away from the obsessive chatter, you'll understand where you are and who's in control. This will help you snap out of those times when you're in a state of emotional chaos.

Since the ghost's mindset is finite, it thinks a subject can be mastered. But mastering something allows you to learn all that there is to know about a subject, and that makes you finite. It puts an end cap on the endless beginning that argues with reality—all of which stunts your growth. In reality, you can never master anything because there's always more to learn. There's an infinite amount of knowledge and experience in any given area. The idea of mastering something is a limiting contradiction that prevents you from seeking more growth. If you think you've mastered something, you act small by playing big (being a master), which is nothing more than you being run by reelality's programming. You think that you are a creator, but you're simply a good actor reading your lines.

Since ghost is manipulative, it will come up with ways to tease us with happiness. For example, my friend Kevin's dog is going through chemotherapy, and even though he's getting great results from it, Kevin won't allow himself to be fully happy.

"I want to be happy, but I also don't want to jinx it," he says.

When ghost is operative, we fear joy, happiness, and love. Ask yourself, when was the last time you wanted to be happy but were scared that if you were, something bad would happen?

Reality is only a friendly universe to the mind that lives and breathes there. For example, we could be sitting in the privacy of our own home where the roof and walls are intact, but when we are focused on a negative thought it feels in our mind as if everything around us is crumbling down. Due to our emotions playing in congruence with our environment, we get triggered in and out of our bodies by way of how we perceive our lives. I've watched entire episodes on TV while sitting next to my husband and not remembered one thing. The stressful reels of what someone did or said or didn't say to me would be all I could see. It would steal my breath away (reelality oxygen) and shrink the room with me in it, quickly squeezing my reality. Then, when I'd turn and ask Chris what happened in the show after it was over, he'd look at me and say, "where were you?"

Oxygen Exists in Reality

Reality and reelality's atmospheres are comparable to earth and space in that reality is thriving in oxygen, which is why when you are in it, you feel happy and healthy. Reelality has more of an anerobic environment (an absence of oxygen), which is why when we are there, life feels like a struggle. This is also why no matter how much we try to breathe our pain away with breath exercises, it won't disappear until we mentally address it (SIT method).

The moment a thought is made into a negatively charged belief we move out of reality and into reelality. Now we are not only trying to survive a negative thought, but we are being operated by it. From the moment the belief becomes absolute, it gains control and has all the power. We feel vulnerable to breathe.

When we fixate on a stressful story, we hold our breath. This places us in a state of resistance where we are unable to receive abundance of any kind. How can we receive love when we believe we are not worthy of it? Thinking and breathing work in unison. Where our minds go, our bodies follow. If we want to be physically healthy, it's important we recognize which atmosphere we are choosing to breathe in. It took me many years to realize that to improve mentally and physically, I had to adjust my thinking. No matter where you go, you take yourself with you. If you're already in a chaotic head space, you will breathe in more of that same environment.

Since energy attracts to where energy is being focused, when we obsess over a negatively charged belief our energy moves mostly to our head. From an energetic standpoint, this removes us from our body. Now we're in our ghost body, in reelality, and in an atmosphere that has little room to breathe. This automatically makes our bodies suffer. Since reelality has little oxygen, I consider it more of an anerobic environment. Breathe all you want, but if you remain ignorant to your negatively charged beliefs, you shall suffer-cate. If you feel triggered and not inspired by this comment or anything else I write, it may be a good time to reflect upon the feeling being conjured. Write it down so that when we get to SIT part two, you'll already have completed step one, which is to find the feeling.

Since there is very little breathable oxygen in *outer space*, we suffocate when we are in reelality. Another way to think about this is when we're fixated on stress, we not only suffer emotionally, but we also suffer physically because we are mostly holding our breaths.

When I go into a movie state of mind, I mentally leave my body, my head floats away like a balloon, and my thinking is negative. Notice how your body reacts when thinking is stressed, how your shoulders pull upwards energetically removing your head from your body, and how your breathing becomes erratic. When our shoulders pull upward, it cuts us off from our heart, which cuts us off from our lungs. Now we're not breathing properly, which also means we're not thinking clearly. The longer we stay like that, the more we suffer.

When our thinking goes viral, so does our life force. This is because thinking and life force energy are intangible. Therefore, where our thinking floats off to, our energy or life force follows it. Whereas when we are not obsessing in our head and are therefore in-reality, life force energy is abundantly flowing throughout us and our bodies are healthy. Happy head, happy body.

Some people believe that breath exercises can help manifest things into their lives, but not in the way one might think. If you need something, it's of great importance to mentally address the need before you breathe so that nothing unwanted is drawn to you. Reality, on the other hand, makes you want for nothing because you already feel emotionally full. This naturally aligns you to receive material things without forcing them to appear. You can still get things from reelality, but since they don't come with the same emotional fullness as reality, you'll be left with wanting more. Force stems from lack, which only produces more lack. This is often the reason why, no matter how much money you may have, it never feels like enough. Reelality does not fill personal voids—it simply reinforces our mental suffering unless it's being used as a tool to *see it through*.

Knowing What You Feel and Think

Take a moment to pause right now and adjust your thinking by relaxing your physical body. Start with the muscles in your face, neck, and shoulders and work your way down. Notice how much more willing you become, how much more open and receptive you feel. This is a great way to allow your mind to open to the underlying issue at hand. It opens the door for you to better hear your pain. When we feel physically relaxed, we automatically begin to breathe better, and this gives our brain more of what it needs to focus and think clearly.

Furthermore, when we relax our mind, our physical body mimics that. While we're amidst emotional or physical stress (like say during a balance pose in yoga class or while running) and our shoulders are relaxed, we're more able to experience the resistance and are more willing to accept it. Relaxing our bodies is a great precursor to being more aware of how we feel. When we're busy distracting ourselves, we're less aware of how we feel. In part two of the SIT method, we'll discover the benefits that can come from using movement and sound to help us access and heal our pain.

When I first began instructing yoga, there were times the studio sound system didn't work and I was forced to lead the class without music. All eyes were now on me to say something interesting or spiritually profound. At least that was the narrative in my head, which made me feel as though I were standing in a naked dream.

The music was there to help fill up the uncomfortable space in my head. My eyes would pull toward my mid-brow turning me into a Cyclops, exposing all my insecurities. I was no longer in the room with the participants. Instead, I was up on center stage with the self that I loathed and feared. The self that made me doubt and overthink everything about myself. My mouth became dry and I found myself struggling to breathe, unable to catch a real breath. I floated above my body, looking down at all the reasons why I was not going to be accepted for what I had to say.

Back then, I would say things I thought the participants wanted to hear. The fear of being judged and not accepted is real only to the one being driven by their negatively charged beliefs, and that was me until my mid-30s. When I found and trusted my voice, I entered class connected to myself and everyone around me. I was in reality and I didn't feel the need to fill space. Trusting what I had to say put me in a position of feeling self-supported, and I discovered that it allowed those around me to do the same.

If I enter a room with the intention to be there for others first, that same codependent energy will be what is projected. That mindset takes energy away from people. You're either a battery giving power or a device consuming power, like a remote control. Showing up authentically for ourselves generates life and can inspire and encourage those around you to do the same without needing them to change so you can feel better. When we are there for others first, it's chiefly because we seek acceptance. That not only makes us struggle more but it makes everyone around us want to do the same.

For a long time, I noticed how every physical activity I participated in involved music. It was there in my breath sessions, at the gym, in my vehicle, and in the yoga classes I attended and instructed. I began to realize that the only reason I pulled in outer sounds is because I didn't like what I was thinking. If I enjoyed my inner conversations, I wouldn't have needed to put on a podcast each time I got into my car and listened to someone else's thinking.

For the first five years of marriage, I disliked my thinking so much that I believed I needed my husband to say and do things to make me feel loved—whether it was a verbal compliment or a physical connection. This kind of ignorant thinking is everywhere in our lives. If we don't like our thoughts, we need not only our spouses to fulfill us, but our bosses, co-workers, friends, family members, and sometimes even complete strangers. The outside world is always showing us our ignorance and what we do not acknowledge in ourselves.

Take a moment to turn down all outer sounds. Do not close your eyes and shut off the outside world. Instead, let the world you're sitting in penetrate and pay attention to how the silence makes your skin feel. Silence has a sound to it that, if you choose to listen, can make or break you. When the volume in your head is cranked up, silence can make you feel restless and anxious. This only makes you want to turn the outside volume louder.

Turn up the sound of your breath or the sound of music so that you don't have to listen to your uncomfortable thinking. Does that make sense to you? Until you like you're thinking, you'll always be looking for things to distract and motivate you. Music is motivating only when you believe you are unmotivating. Later we will discover how when we unconditionally accept the volume in our heads, we remove old conditioning and, in its place, receive new understandings that can lead to an overall, quieter atmosphere.

Pay close attention to your career, finances, relationships, and health. Are you happy in all, or only a few areas of your life? The question should help you see where you are and what kind of air you breathe during those times. This will also help you to realize when you need approval or are without your phone or music. Why do you need external stimuli to feel supported?

In answering these questions, we see ourselves and discover whether we like who we are. The only way out is in. To feel good in our skin and not need other people's approval to motivate us, we must first sit still in outer silence. The volume in our heads will be turned up loud enough for us to do something if we want it bad enough.

Breath Work is Only Part of the Solution

Some of the things I share may not work for you, which is understandable. As I said before, this book is more a sharing than a telling. When we breathe in reelality we suffer, whereas when we breathe in reality, we flourish.

I used to believe that for me to flourish mentally and physically meant I had to spend between 15 minutes to an hour daily on breathwork. Sometimes I'd use a variety of different yoga breathing techniques. Other times I would simply sit and focus on my in and out breaths, similar to a form of meditation. Adding a breath routine to your schedule is not a bad thing—I'm simply highlighting where you might be breathing. If you need to set aside time to breathe, ask yourself why you must do so and why your normal breathing does not give that to you? If you don't feel good beforehand and still do it, you're deflecting from problems and are therefore reinforcing being held captive in reelality. The longer you're there, the more ignorant of your thinking you become.

Reelality makes us forget where our point of power is (reality) and this robs you of oxygen. This is why some of us believe we must complete breath exercises. Breathing exercises will not snap you out of anything but will instead keep you hypnotized. While they may make you feel better temporarily, when you wake up in the morning or get home from work, you will tell yourself you need to do it again since you're not dealing with what's really going on inside of you.

The mind and the breath work in unison. The more you deflect and use things to compound that deflection, the more you need them. This is the reason why so many people drink at the end of their day. It helps take the edge off, but it doesn't solve anything. Whether you're breathing, exercising, or drinking to avoid yourself, you still wake up with the same kind of hungover thinking. You may tell yourself you're making healthier choices in your life, but are you really? It takes a still mind to recognize all that needs to be seen. Ignorance hides—that's why it's defined as unawareness or obliviousness.

You have found your way to this book, and it may be because you've come to realize that no matter how much you breathe, or workout, or eat right, nothing has changed on an emotional level. Ask yourself what body you want to keep coming back to—one that is on life support or a body that thrives on reality.

Addressing my mental distress provides me with trust, and that gives me power. The more I establish feeling emotionally centered (something that happens when we SIT), the less frazzled and emotionally wobbly I feel when I return to my body after being triggered out of it. We all bump into stress throughout our lives. I've found when I mentally work my way through my mental struggles, they do not control me as they once did. I still experience stress, but it no longer kicks me out of my body for as long of a time. This is important, as the longer we are removed from our physical bodies (absentminded), the less we can remember. The less we remember, the more we forget where in reality our physical bodies are.

For some, the longer they are gone the more panicky and depressed they feel. For others, they become unaffected to the point where they're unaware that anything's wrong. When their bodies show them what has gone on, they feel surprised.

Throughout my 13-year career as a yoga facilitator, I tried many different types of breath exercises, but they all felt like too much work. Dedicating time each day to doing something that my body already had the natural ability to do was frustrating at best.

I wanted to be able to breathe well all the time, or at least more of the time, without having to force my breath. This is why I now hold myself accountable for things that make me uncomfortable. Through the vehicle of experience, I understand that breath exercises won't eliminate those things for me. If I want to feel better, I must spend more time in reality, period. The body follows the mind, and therefore, it makes sense that the only way out of a stressful situation is the same way I fell into it: through my thinking.

To embody a better quality of air, you must first move into a better mental facility that thrives with reality oxygen.

Chapter 5

"SEA-ING" YOURSELF THROUGH THE SCRIPT

Reality unfolds life as it is, whereas reelality is a superimposed argument that disallows life to happen as it is. Reality provides us with free will. Reelality makes us feel we must fight for success, our relationships, our rights and equality. Often it can also make us feel as though we are trapped in our thinking. If we stand in resistance to situations in life, we are in reelality. We are being influenced by the ghost, and the longer we stay in its astral existence, the harder it will be to climb out. Nonetheless, all this means is that we require greater understanding at a more concentrated level of the negative side of the battery. By implication, our understanding when fully resolved will be profound.

Electricity

If you're unhappy with the present, your view remains blocked by an emotionally unresolved past. The physical body resembles a battery with a positive charge on top and a negative charge on the bottom, creating an electromagnetic field around us. Soul resides everywhere, including the top of our bodies. The reason it does not interfere with the ghost's world is due to free will. To interfere would defeat the purpose of our growth here in these physical bodies.

Negatively charged beliefs are semiconscious up until we have seen our way through them, which is what we do when we SIT. This is why when they're active, we are also semiconscious. When we *See It Through*, we are unconditionally accepting the negative charge (which is the story we've built up around the feeling) and because of that, combine both sides of the battery. This gives our physical bodies vitality and longevity—something science is unable to see. Over time, the more we SIT the more we unconditionally accept *all* of ourselves and realize there are no negative parts of ourselves, only clarity or confusion.

Doubt holds and emits an electrical charge that produces an electromagnetic field that attracts other fields like it. An electromagnetic field is an emotionally chaotic headspace. When we have a genuine positive thought all electrical charges shut off. This allows us to connect with one another on a real level (reality) not a reel/pretend one where we are putting up a false persona of ourselves. Doubt keeps us apart and trust brings us together. Some believe these fields surround us all the time. I would agree but only when we are in a state of mistrust. When we doubt, our mental state becomes prickly, which sometimes can make our bodies feel prickly.

Take a moment and think back to the last time you doubted yourself or someone else. How did it make your skin feel? Was it hot or irritated? What about the last time someone gave you a bad vibe? Did the thought make the hairs on your neck and arms stand up? Now that I've mentioned this to you, you may be more likely to notice the next time, and when you do, you'll know that you've put your electrical guard up and are doubting something.

When we trust, we deactivate the negative charge surrounding the belief. We no longer feel electrocuted by our stressful thoughts.

Science sees electricity in everything, including in us. Science puts things into boxes so it cannot "sea" (connect) to anything real. All it sees is the reel (measurement).

As a society we have been taught to believe that our physical bodies are electrically wired just like we have been taught to believe that we age, get sick, and die. These concepts all hold and emanate a negative charge that we condition ourselves to believe and then pass on to the next generation. I'm not saying that science is wrong. I agree with it, but I'm also sharing my opinion of how I believe we become electrical.

Take a moment to reflect upon how you felt mentally and physically the last time you were stressed. Stressful thoughts can send title waves of uncomfortable and even painful or electrifying sensations throughout the body. We then react to these sensations mentally and *it* goes until we either see our way through it or we keep suppressing it to the point where we go numb to it. Now, because stress has become our normal, it takes something dramatic to stress us out. When we see our way through emotional turmoil, positive and negative combine and our bodies become electrically neutral. We no longer feel emotionally prickly.

I mentioned, it's my opinion that we are only electrical when we are in a state of resistance. This is true for most people most of the time. We're in resistance anytime we measure something or someone. Science is unable to see non-resistance or potential because it's measuring its subject. Since science puts it subjects into a box, its thinking is the box. Having said that, doubt puts us into a box on purpose to create purpose. Without walls, we wouldn't feel the charge or motivation to want to figure our way out of the box. Exploring the box is the journey of our Soul's evolution here in these physical bodies. Feeling confined, conditional, and judgmental helps us unravel and become. Our trying to figure the box or life out allows us to go in and start to know ourselves.

Reality is peaceful, which is why when we are there it appears as a friendly universe. Reality manifests whereas reelality materializes. Reality allows life to unfold through unconditional acceptance, and it's through unconditional acceptance that we receive life. Reelality does not receive, at least not without hard work involved. When we are manifesting, things come to us naturally. We don't have to try and make things come to us like we do in reelality like we might with visualization and meditation techniques. Both avenues try to bend and manipulate the laws of cause and effect to get what they want (something I'll touch more on later when explaining Law of Attraction). Due to the emotional information going outwards, when we don't trust ourselves, we're unable to effortlessly receive. Everything we want in life feels like a struggle. When our lives are being materialized, life is being decided for us because the programming is controlling our perception of reality. Therefore, life feels hard.

DNA

I used the word *materialize* to describe reelality because when there, we're being run by the script (which can either be our DNA, ancestral script, or our own programming). The DNA contains our ancestral lineage. When we are born into human form, we enter with a prewritten set of instructions. We think we are living our lives, but for the most part, we're reacting to our parents and grandparents programming. We think we're forming our own opinions, but we're not. It isn't until later when some of us wake up to wanting a better-quality life that we become more aware that we're veering off script. The less comatose we are to our thinking, the more cognizant we become when a thought that opposes reality enters in.

Often when our thinking changes, so too does our environment and the people in it. Some of us find ourselves diving even deeper into self-explorations in search of alternative medicines that lead us to various healers, shamans, etc.

This is also how some of us may assemble new families. For me, as a by-product of self-acceptance, I met a lot of great friends that became like my family. This is how we create a new healthy family and leave the old family that we are no longer lining up with where they are. Just because people happen to be blood relatives does not mean that they are Soul family. The more we uncover and discover from an accepting standpoint in ourselves, the more we align to people doing the same thing for themselves.

Throughout these endeavors, it's important we remain aware of how the ghost can prevent us from getting well. For example, some of us will choose healers that make us feel comfortable (what feels familiar but isn't necessarily supportive). Healers that have a certain look, age, or gender. And yet, it's what makes us feel the most uncomfortable that we want to explore because that is where the resistance is.

Over time, the more negatively charged beliefs we expose and resolve, the less controlled by the ancestral script we become. We start writing our own scripts, becoming life livers and conscious creators. We are no longer being acted out. When our DNA is running us, it means we are on autopilot (hypnotized) to the script reeling out of us. We read our lines like an actor does. The longer we remain in character the harder it is to wake up from the act.

Since we enter this life with a prewritten set of instructions, we get good at following other people's instructions. We get in line and do as we are told because that's what so many of us are already used to doing rather than asking questions like is this food or medicine or information good for me? If the TV or government says it's good for me, it must be true. We don't pause to realize its someone else's truth.

Having said all that, what's paramount for us to understand is that we are the ancestral lineage. Our ancestors unfold from the same loin we do. They are us. When we use the script as an excuse to dump our problems, it's like saying "my problems aren't mine, I inherited them." It bolsters ignorance, which bolsters lack of self-acceptance. Where there is lack today, there is lack from all our yesterdays. This is how victimized material (which are conversations and actions that, when activated by us, create and confirm circumstances in our environments), gets passed down to us. The energy, from one victimized conversation pulls on others like it—both from this life and previous ones (I say previous but since I believe all time happens simultaneously, there's no such thing as past) that then reel out of us covering reality, rendering us reality blind.

So, when we choose to remain asleep in one life by not addressing that our pain today is also being passed on from the lives before it, we pass it on to the next life. But when we heal the pain we feel from our past in this time zone, light fills in to seal the astral gap between all our previous lives (light in this example representing self-acceptance). Therefore, *all* time collapses and we are no longer controlled by a mostly unconscious past. At the same time, we are not karmically bound to other lifetimes like some may believe. There's no such thing as karma when you're in the timeless. We can choose right now not to bring these patterns with us into the next day, next year, or next life when we're willing to *see them through*.

All DNA contain disease codes like Alzheimer's, dementia, and cancer and are pre-written within us. These diseases don't become active until our re-action to something in our environment switches it on. For example, the more I refuse to accept my anxiety, the more it will show up in my environment. I will eventually be presented with a certain circumstance that will activate a gene that is vibrational and therefore an emotional match to it. The gene—a part of the scripts material—would materialize a physical experience for me when triggered to feel and either unconditionally accept (and therefore process and move on) or further deny and possibly die from.

Until we fundamentally alter what pains us today, our past will continue to override us, because the past is with us now. It's in our mind, and therefore it's in our blood. The more we SIT, the more we change our minds and our DNA. We deactivate the negative charges holding our feelings hostage and no longer feel like victims that attract victim-like situations.

Healing Self, Not Changing Others

Something to keep in mind is that just because we decide to change doesn't mean everyone else around us needs to change too. All that does is create more denial to recover from. If I think you need to be where I am, I must not be where I think I am. Remember, the ghost is conniving. Its job is to keep you outside of your body away from reality so that it can stay relevant.

When we turn into a ghost, it's because we've left the building and are now out of our bodies acting conditional, looking for people who are on the same emotional wavelength, to control. Whereas when we are in our body's reality, we trust who we are and don't feel the need to control our environment and everything in it.

What's happening in our bodies is a micro to the macro earth. When we treat our body well, the earth reflects that back to us. Having said that, when we are in our ghost body, we think the world revolves around us. If I believe those around me must do what I'm doing to take care of my health, I'm a slave to my environment. When I take care of my body, I don't need others to follow suit. I understand that mindset keeps me from seeing light in others, and since what we see in others is our own reflection, I can see when I'm in the dark.

This brings me back to something I said earlier in a roundabout way. The difference between *thinking* you know something versus knowing it. When we *know*, it's because we trust who and where we are. We live in a friendly universe and don't need others to change. In reality, we understand that taking care of our individual mind and body is something that radiates from the inside-out. We understand that it's our perception that changes the environment, not what other people do or don't do.

What you think lays the foundation upon which you walk. So, if you question whether you can trust a certain person or situation but do nothing to address the underlying scratch that's making you mistrust in the first place, where does that leave you? Eventually you continue to create additional scenarios in your mind that lead to more doubt. The more you blame others for how you feel the more you avoid reality, and the less you can connect to the outside world.

All relationships are here to show us how to grow together, not push us further apart. But since many of us stay fixated on the outer environment being separate from us, we miss the opportunity to grow and evolve from it. People love to point fingers, but that only removes our point of power. If we are unable to see another person trying to help us mitigate an unsatisfactory situation, then we remain a prisoner to it.

When we choose to get high on a negatively charged belief, we feel out of control, and in a way, we are.

The more desensitized we are to reality, the more conditional we become. I will love you *until* you do something I don't like. I can still love you and be mad at you. No matter how hard we try and convince ourselves of that being the truth, it doesn't work that way. You love or you don't. You are unconditional or you are conditional. There is no flip flopping—only the ghost does that.

When I authentically feel connected to myself, I don't feel a resistance to the outside world, which includes you. Because there's no charge between us, we come together and in a way are one. Since doubt activates a negative electrical charge, when I mistrust, I automatically put a wall between us.

This creates a gap between you and me and that makes us separate instead of one.

When I don't trust myself, I'm unable to see us as conduits assisting one another. My perception divides us. You and I can still have two separate physical bodies standing next to one another, but the thing that unbinds us from being one is our frame of mind.

For example, have you ever had a relationship with someone, platonic or intimate, where when you are not seeing eye to eye it almost pains you to go near them? That's static electricity or negative charge. But when the fight is over, the electricity collapses and we automatically want to be near them again.

Nevertheless, the fight would have to be fully resolved (meaning you couldn't be pretending to like the person) for there to be an authentic joining. If there is not, you'd still have your doubts about how you feel and project that onto the other person (which is you having your guard up, similar to how porcupine quills go up when it's in defense mode).

Pretending to be okay in any relationship when you're not hurts—hence the term "love hurts." Love hurts only because conditions are in the way. Conditions are denied feelings. Until we feel our feelings, we will continue to put our hurt and conditions onto others. Later we may say that we were with the wrong partner, but since we emotionally align to one another, we are always with the right partner.

No one can make us feel something that's not already in us. What we emotionally send out is received and brought back to us as a means to help us heal our inner pain. Most of the time this isn't what we think we asked for. That's because pain vibrates louder than desire does. It's been more reinforced by our resistance to not feel over the years and has more concentrated layers driving it.

The person you think you're having trust issues with is the person that responded to your call and is now bringing you exactly what you asked for—an opportunity to reflect and transform unaccepted feelings into accepted ones.

Remember, it's not the other person we don't trust—it's our resistance to feel our feelings that's making us not trust. As mentioned and purposely repeated, when we resist feeling it creates a negative charge around the feeling that we think is the feeling but is not. When I *See It Through* and the charge becomes inactive, there's nothing to fear. Until then, I will continue to feel the charge, and because of that it will oversee me.

When we see the negative charge through, we lift the burden off ourselves and stop making others responsible for our happiness. The people in our lives can come and go as they please, and in doing so, we are genuinely pleased for them.

Until we accept *all* of ourselves, we will continue to attract people that will not accept all of us, which causes our life force to drain from us, rendering our bodies fragile and vulnerable to rapid aging and illness.

We cannot unconditionally accept all of ourselves without lovingly supporting the feelings we fear in others. What we fear in others is a projection reeling out of us, to us, and for us. Without contrast there would be no incentive for us to want to find trust—the dark lives to serve the light. Remaining open to this concept keeps the mind open to want to align both sides of the battery so that our electrically run beliefs no longer frighten us. This is how self-work turns into a self-care routine we look forward to.

When we deny our feelings, we rely on the outer environment and the people in it to make us happy. When they are unable to do that, we blame them and feel worse. Many people think that if they are with the right person, living in the right town, or working the right job, that it'll make them happy. If their dream job doesn't make them happy, they blame the job and start looking for a new one. The reality is, happiness, like other emotional fulfillment, comes from within. Denying that leads to blaming others and circumstances for our unhappiness. This is true of other emotions as well, and it's an endless cycle of unfulfillment.

Yet it is through one another (co-creation) that we access our inner freedom. Without the other person helping to confirm our denial (by showing us what we are lacking inside when we try to blame them), it's harder to see what's hidden in us. Ignorance makes us reality blind. Just because we think we've done the self-work and have evolved or changed doesn't mean we have. If the environment keeps giving you heartache, it's because there's still denial that requires understanding. I'm not saying we can't reflect upon the same things on our own because some of us can. We just might not be able to do it in the same way. There's a reason we're all here together and not standing on our own. When we seize the opportunity to access our feelings through one another, over time, we feel less defensive. In turn, because we are more receptive to listening (mental body) our physical bodies are receptive to repair mode and healing.

Human Magnets

Life will always show us where we are emotionally lacking by way of who and what are standing before us. When we really take notice, we can find our own peace with that *thrown* or hurt part of ourselves rather than blame the other person or circumstance. Many of us will have a hard time accepting this. I know I certainly did. Whether it's the victim or the martyr running you, it will do its best to stay relevant. This is why it's important to understand that when you don't shine light onto it, it will feel unmovable. When something feels unmovable it's because it has very little consciousness. Therefore, when we don't do our best to move it, which is to *see it out*, we remain unconscious and unmovable with it.

If we want to spot what's hidden, we must be willing to look at our sticky parts—the parts hiding behind the aspects of ourselves we believe are relevant. In other words, look at everything that feels unmoveable in yourself, every crevasse requires justification. Ask yourself where you feel victimized in your life, and who triggers it. Still your mind and go there for a moment. If you can't find feeling victimized, find where you might be making someone else feel victimized. Whose life are you trying to control? Who are you belittling and not supporting? Who irritates and or makes you angry?

If we want to get off the victim reel and not attract reasons to feel that way, we've got to be willing to reflect. Otherwise, the script keeps running and we remain asleep, being lived instead of living life.

What we give to ourselves, we will receive more of.

People love to say they created or manifested something great into their life when something great appears but want no responsibility for it when it's not good. The reason why we sometimes can't figure out how we attracted such a terrible event and or person into our lives is because we didn't arrange the event or person.

Let me explain. The vibration of doubt and whatever else is attached to it (and there's always lower frequencies attached to it like fear, guilt, anger, rage etc.) are active in us, whether we are conscious of it or not. Which is why we can sometimes be shocked at what happens or comes back to us. In other words, we may not be aware of the suppressed rage that's attached to doubt and attract someone or a situation that reflects rage because the frequency of rage is speaking the loudest. It's the frequency of the emotions that determine the outcome. The information goes out, and when it does, we're not in control of who answers it. We're not in control of what they will say or do or how the circumstance of events will unfold.

Since many of us are oblivious or numb to how we really feel, we also don't realize what we're emitting and calling back to us. Let's not forget there's also the ancestral script that's running and can also be calling in energies we're not aware of until they are right in front of us. So, when something bad happens, don't be hard on yourself and say "I created that" even though in a roundabout way you as a whole (DNA), did.

Until we accept all of ourselves, and that includes everything that comes our way by seeing our way through all of it, whether we are conscious of having a part in it or not, we will continue to blame the outside world and remain a victim. If what I just said triggers you write your feelings down so that when we get to the SIT method part 2 in the next chapter you'll have something to possibly, if willing, work your way through. Remember, this sharing is meant to assist you in using the *outer* as a means to look at yourself.

Another thing that keeps the victim reel in us running is sharing our sad stories with one another. The ghost does this to dump its emotional weight onto others. In the process, it keeps itself relevant. If we believe telling our sad stories helps us to relate and is a way for us to connect, we know where our head is at and what is in charge of us.

Sharing our sad stories is not a bad thing. They can be a catalyst to help someone see something painful through in their own lives. But there's a difference between sharing and dumping. When you're caught on a victim reel and it's all you can talk about day after day, year after year, to everyone and anyone who will listen, that's dumping and not helping. Also as mentioned, our bodies download every word we speak to ourselves, and those words hold and emit vibrations that are the tuning forks to our physical realities. What we think and talk about most becomes physical and lays the foundation upon which we walk and experience.

So, if you tell sad stories from a place where there's no real emotional resolve, you won't be helping anyone—especially not yourself, and what you're resisting will persist. Whereas when we apply ourselves to seeing our pain through, we don't feel compelled to dump the victim story and instead talk more about the victory story. This sometimes consists of a back story to give clarity on where we are today and sometimes not. Sometimes the past won't come up in conversations as it might have normally before—not because we're trying to avoid it but because we feel we've worked through it. Since our bodies have downloaded that information and made a record of it, it's now a reflex we react to. The story no longer feels relevant to tell and is now replaced with a story of where we are right now. Pause for a moment to ask yourself where you are telling your sad stories from. Is it a place of harmony or disharmony?

When we see a negative charge through, we're no longer trying to drag someone else down with us. People that project their unwellness onto others often want the same unwellness projected back onto them. The monster needs feeding. Over time, emotional darkness can become addictive, and when the addiction is not *seen through*, it can lead to an overdose called physical violence.

Being Emotionally Charged

The experience brings the understanding.

We now know that emotions are vibrational. We all have an inner energy field that radiates outward and connects to a collective field (other people's emotional energy fields). Our outer environment is an emotional projection that stems from within all of us. Another way to think about this is what we sense outside of us is a by-product and combination of everyone's emotions. If we all understood this, the war out there would be seen much differently. We would know our lives were being arranged based off our feelings. The desire to hold grudges would be non-existent. Over the years I've heard people say they already know this. But if they truly did, they wouldn't be complaining about their families, friends, or coworkers. Instead, they would be taking ownership of the feeling's others were triggering in them and doing something within themselves to resolve it.

I mentioned how when we refuse to accept our feelings, we also refuse to accept our Souls purpose, which is to have a human experience and feel everything. For us to feel everything, we need the assistance of an outer experience to inspire the feeling into motion. This is what we are doing when we get triggered or inspired to feel our emotions (it's a trigger or an inspiration depending upon how we are perceiving our situation).

Without experience, information sits on the surface layer of our mental body and acts like a shield. It remains something learned but not known. To think we know something because we've read a book or two on the subject only adds more conditional layers, preventing us from hearing new information.

My stepfather once said to me (because he was a drug and alcohol addiction counselor) "If you were a drug addict who would you rather have as your counselor, someone who went to school and studied drug addiction but never had a drug problem or someone who did have a drug problem but turned their life around and now has the life-experience and education to pass that information to you?"

Anytime we doubt, we move away from trust. We put on an electromagnetic shield (electromagnetic field) over our common sense, which our inner sense understands as instinct. We are blocked from reality by the shield. It possesses outer senses, or our one sense (instinct) that's broken into multiple senses (taste, touch, smell, hearing, and sight). When our thinking is scattered so too are our senses, leaving us reality-senseless and reelality-sensitive.

The longer a person remains hypnotized, the more electrically charged their electromagnetic shield grows. This makes them think they're feeling sensitive when they're only being held hostage in their electrically wired head. When we're emotionally sensitive, it's because we're captivated by a negatively charged belief running us. It's doing so because of our ignorance to it. Lack of responsibility and accountability to feel puts the issue in charge of us. The more oblivious we are to our reactions, the more charged the shield becomes, numbing us to our true feelings (instinct).

We know if we're being electrically controlled because we won't be able to take in our outside world. We will filter information, making some right and some wrong. We will be unable to hear what people are saying (whether on TV, radio, or directly in front of us) without feeling an offensive reaction to it. Politics are a good example of this.

When we see our way through pain, we're not sensitive to anything anyone says to us. We take advantage of the outer by using it as a way to reflect.

Protests are excuses to deflect from accepting responsibility for our feelings. If someone calls you fat, weak, or troubled and you get angry at them rather than reflect upon the feeling stemming from the trigger, the denial only digs you a deeper hole into your misery. If instead we SIT, we realize it was never the comment that got our backs up—it was the charge holding the feeling hostage that did.

The more we deny in ourselves, the more *outer space* fills in and widens the astral gap between mind and body and you and me. The more we SIT the more light fills in and closes the gap. To become non-reactive to any comment, we must first allow ourselves-to react. The trigger is the helper to gain access to the feeling. Then we can turn our attention toward unconditionally accepting the feeling and allowing the feeling to tell its story through us. This way, we deactivate the negative charge and automatically feel less sensitive to want to react.

Whether its emotional or physical, stress can become our normal to the point where, unless something dramatic happens, we remain unaware of our state of mind. When I was bartending in my 20s, I was asked, like many bartenders, to work 18- to 20-hour days for 10 days in a row during stampede week (an annual rodeo, exhibition, and festival held every July in Calgary). I managed to pull through for three summers, however during the last year of my bartending career I fell over and passed out. I was taken by ambulance to the hospital for dehydration and exhaustion. I was running on stress fumes for months before that but was unaware of it until I collapsed.

Today, thanks to the SIT, I'm more able to innately feel and spot the reflection of my own mental unwellness staring back at me sooner, allowing me to tackle it before it tackles me. The more I choose to work through my own fearful paranoid feelings, the more the environment arranges for me ways for fearful and exhausting situations and events not to be in my life anymore.

"Sea-ing"

So, as mentioned, the portrait of life starts from the inside. It gets projected outward like a film reel that's then reflected outward to you. How you choose to see this picture is always up to you, even when following someone else's advice. You either see life and all its contents or "sea" it. I believe "to see" means that you're on autopilot watching your life more from a sideline position. You have handed the reins over to your programming (beliefs) and now they're making all decisions. You're not engaging with reality but, instead, are a consequence of reelality. Conversely when you "sea," you are connected to reality and therefore are an extension of it. Your eyes are open, and life is allowed in as you are not conflicted by the past. Because the past does not define authentically who you are today, it's unable to block your view of reality. Remember, reelality superimposes images over reality so that you cannot see it.

When some people look out on the world, they're conflicted with what's pictured back. Rather than a friendly universe, they see war, disease, poverty, and even conspiracy. Sea represents water, and consciousness is symbolic of water. When we're not being controlled by our negatively charged beliefs, our internal flow is not stagnant as it is when we "see." We are in a merge with all bodies of water and no longer swimming in small ponds, having connected with the ocean that connects to all oceans. This view allows us to be among everyone's perspective, not merely our own.

When you're not busy arguing against the outer world as an entity outside of you, it's allowed in by you, and the fight stops. If we all truly knew that the world exists for us from the inside out, we would likely be more accountable for our actions.

Another reason I shared my explanation of sea was to shed light upon how when we SIT, we tune not just our minds, but also our physical bodies to become more conscious. When we submerse ourselves in water, some of us find more clarity. Ever notice how some of your best ideas surface when you're in the shower or bathtub? That's because when water runs over the physical body it also runs over our electrically charged field, temporarily deactivating it. This is also why we sometimes receive a thought from our gut (instinct) that helps us solve a problem, but within minutes of getting out of the shower, the static electricity field fires back up again and we forget. I keep a pad and pen in my bathroom to avoid situations like this from happening.

Water is alive and is its own beingness. It's a generator, accelerator, conductor and promoter of life. All life originates in water—from the very earliest life forms to evolve to growing embryos in a womb or egg. Water, when you're open to it, acts as a vehicle to not only hear all life but communicate with it. This includes all ecosystems, plants, and minerals as well as planets and universes because they too are alive and are their own entities.

I'm going to close by saying for us to decide where we want to go in life, we must unconditionally accept both the positive and negative parts of ourselves. It's the only way we will come to understand what our purpose here in these physical bodies is and be able to understand and know who we are.

Chapter 6

SIT METHOD PART TWO

You cannot be the creator of your own reality until you accept *all* of yourself. Without full acceptance of feeling, the ghost will remain the host.

When we unconditionally accept *all* of ourselves, our bodies light up from the inside out (which to me, is what the Christ body is) and we unite with others rather than fight with them. When we unconditionally accept the feelings that are overriding us today from our past, we collapse time. Therefore, time is no longer in charge of us. Unconditionally accepting the negative side of the battery aligns us to the positive, and when we combine both sides (which is what we do when we SIT), we deactivate the charge holding the feeling hostage. We no longer feel like a prisoner to our past, and the past no longer dictates who we are today.

According to reality, there's no such thing as the past, present, or future. Instead, there's only the timeless or eternal beginning. That is why, when we are there with it, we don't struggle. When we are not trying to get away from the past to get to the future, we stand still and embody emotional lightness. This promotes bodily light, which surpasses the speed of light and collapses time which collapses measurement which collapses you and me being separate from one another.

Until we go back to SIT with our burdened pasts, they will continue to keep controlling us today and tomorrow because, as mentioned, the more we try to walk away from our pain the more it persists. I couldn't be free of women hurting me until I healed my mother pain from the past.

The SIT method allows us to see how, when we resist accepting all our feelings, we also resist our Soul's purpose, which is to embody and embrace being human. Therefore, we resist God which in turn makes us need a God, spouse, employer, friend, or stranger to not only save us, but be what defines who we are.

There are many layers to each of these steps. Some have been explained already and others may require further explanation, which is what the latter half of this chapter will entail. As you already know, there are some things I purposely repeat as a means to help you remember. While some of these things you will have already heard and others not, always pay attention to how you feel as you are reading and take the time to be still with whatever comes up, as it will help you understand yourself that much better.

Before starting I want to remind you that I'm not a trained therapist, nor do I have a degree in medicine. This book is a sharing, not a telling. So, like anything you read, pay attention to how you feel and don't do anything that does not align to your wellbeing or the wellbeing of others. If you are taking medication for depression or any other mental disorder, it's important that you talk with a health care professional to assess what SIT method, if any, is right for you.

SIT 2

Find a safe, comfortable environment—preferably alone in your home so that you won't be disturbed, unless you feel it's necessary to have someone there to supervise like a friend, family member, or therapist. If you're able, set aside at least an hour. Ghost loves distractions and will look for any reason to get out of feeling. We cannot unconditionally accept anything when we are in a conditional mind.

1. *Find the feeling*: To access the feeling, you can use the story as ammunition.

2. *Sound and movement*: What does the feeling sound and or move like? This exercise does not encourage dramatic acting out. Align yourself to authentic sound and or movement. For example, cry, moan, sob, scream, yell, shake, quiver, roll around. Vibrate your body with the emotion as it comes out.

3. *Unconditionally accepting the feeling*: Allow the feeling and whatever else comes with it, be that sound or movement to safely be as big as it wants to be, without judgment or condition. As we will sooner discover, judgement and condition do not allow movement. If you have guilt that requires feeling, you may need to feel nothing or numbness first. Exhaust the feeling, allow the feeling to occupy your body and mind. This is not about losing your mind. It's about allowing your emotions to flow so that old conditioning is replaced with new understandings. When we see our feelings through, we get to understand them. This helps us to figure out where they fit in our lives.

4. An example to closing a SIT (optional): It's safe to feel my feelings. It feels good to feel my feelings. I love my feelings. Thank you, feelings, etc.

Find the Feeling

So, first thing we do when we SIT is find the feeling, which won't be difficult when we're being triggered into it. If you're not being triggered into it, forcing yourself to feel an emotion on your own can be challenging, though not impossible. For example, if I'm out in public with friends or family or I'm at work and I find myself being triggered but am not able to SIT with the emotion where I am, I'll grab my phone and make a list of the feelings I'm feeling. I'll also explain who triggered them and why. This is where we meditate. When we traditionally meditate, we observe how we feel rather than react to the feeling. Think of it this way: we do outer work when we go to work and when we get home, we do Soul work.

Sound and Movement

All feelings have sound. Since sound carries vibration, when we make sound, it moves the feelings, which then allows us to emotionally process those feelings—though it's not necessary to do either. But if you feel stuck, making sound can often help get emotions moving and you feel more in touch with them. Another thing I found helped me to access my feelings is letting all sound in. If there are sounds going on around you (like say the sound of traffic outside your window), instead of letting it be a distraction that pulls you out of the SIT, see it as an extension of yourself. Remember, life starts from the inside out. I've realized during some of my SITs, that the more I *let all sound in*, the more sound comes out. I don't try to fight the head chatter, I allow it and use it as ammunition to access my feelings.

Once you have found the feeling, ask yourself, "What does this feeling sound like?" and "What would this feeling possibly move like?" If nothing comes out, you may want to make up a sound you think sounds like the emotion or moves like it. I have found this helps massage those deeper layers up to the surface where they then become more authentic sounds. Whatever sound comes out, embrace it without placing conditions on it. In other words, don't tell yourself you're being too loud or not loud enough.

Attaching sound to feeling isn't just something I do when I SIT. When I have an emotion bubble up, if I'm in an environment where I feel safe to express it, I will. I rarely make loud sounds out in public, but if a moan or a sigh wants to come out and I'm not in the vicinity of disturbing anyone, I will let it out. When I'm at home or driving in my car, sometimes sounds will be louder. I don't force these sounds.

If in the beginning, you might feel resistance to making sound. Don't force yourself because that too, is conditional. If you feel resistance about making sound, become aware of the feeling that's preventing you from making the sound. The resistance to make sound may be the feeling you're working with at that time. These may be more than the feelings you originally thought you were working on. You might think you're working on one feeling but then it shifts to a totally different feeling that leads you to other people, places, and situations that had nothing to do with what you thought you were *sitting* with in the first place. Words hold us outside of the feeling.

Try not to use words during this process because words have either a positive or negative charge around them. The reason for not speaking positive words is because just like the negative, they can create an imbalance that steers us away from the actual feeling and focuses more on the behaviour pattern we've instilled into the word. These may have many other words attached to it too that ultimately lead us to why we came up with the positive in the first place, because we don't like feeling negative or bad. It can be easy to bypass how we really feel when fixated on the story. This is why during this process, we initially only use the story to inspire the feeling into action, then to access the feeling ask ourselves "what does this feeling sound like."

And so, we want to go beyond the words to the sound of the feeling. That way we have less chance of getting held hostage and captivated by the charge when we do access the feeling. SIT 2 is about allowing ourselves to get in touch with our emotions and feel our way through them.

Words can become bigger and more absolute than the sound. Stories can deter us from feeling because it's easy to get sucked back into the reels of the story line, pulling us in multiple directions. Sound brings life and vibration back into the cells of our bodies, reminding and sometimes even awakening us to remember other languages from other lifetimes. In my memory, this sounded similar to whale language. I have also heard music that I have never heard before—musical instruments that felt like they were coming out of my heart.

Ask yourself, "What does your emotional or physical pain sound like versus what's its story?"

During my yoga classes, I would often sing my own chants rather than repeating someone else's chant because it felt more natural to me. Trust your own voice. Remember, you are your own repairer. You save you. When you forget that priceless piece of information, you find yourself dependant on someone else's words, which seek and need outer compliments and approvals. Unorganized pain seeks to be saved, whereas organized pain does not. This does not mean that other people's chants cannot be healing, because they can. When we authentically want to feel better, we align to other people's sounds in a way that does not separate us from them. When we don't see them as an extension of something coming from us, back to us, and are conduits to one another, we strengthen the gap between you and me.

Now, one of us is big and the other is small. When we are in alignment with ourselves, singing other people's chants can act like tuning forks to hear our own sounds and chants, which can inspire us to live in our truth. They can pre-pave the way for us to be able to hear ourselves. This is similar to the time when I traveled around the world and had certain people use their modalities on me. I didn't go to these people to learn and then mimic what they knew. I went to them because a part of me knew that it is was through what they had to offer that I'd be able to hear and know my own gifts and inner talents more distinctly.

Parents can also make this a fun and freeing experience for their children. When your kids are fighting with one another or are stressed out in anyway and you find yourself stressed out in believing you need to save them, invite them to *SIT* with their feelings. Encourage them (while under your supervision) to get out of the story and into their feelings by asking them what does your feeling sound or move like. Inspire them to be their own repairers and saviours. Give them a safe place so that they can express themselves, and in doing so, feel free from *it*.

Think of it this way—sound speaks to the Soul whereas words speak to the ghost. Nothing creates fear more than war, and how do we create war? We create it by not *seeing it through*. We create war by incessantly arguing in our heads and arguing with other people, getting stuck on negatively charged story loops. So, *all* fear starts in our thinking and radiates out into the world and throughout our physical body. As we will soon discover, this causes our bodies to be in an inflamed state. Our thinking literally gives us physical inflammation, which I believe to be the seed of all disease. The SIT method helps us to become less inflamed in our thinking, which in turn makes a sounder mind.

There are times where I find myself making a lot of sound and movement and other times, none. I found that during the first six months of my experiences with SIT part two, I made a lot of sound and sometimes, movement. This organically shifted into me making very little sound and no movement.

I'm not suggesting that no movement is an evolved state. I'm simply explaining what has taken place for me. For me, no movement has been incredibly powerful. I have found that what I considered physical pain or even slight irritations (like wanting to scratch an ich) that I don't engage with turn into relaxed, pleasurable, and even orgasmic sensations. I've also realized that it was the movement that led me to stillness. Yes, I practice yoga and go to the gym and walk my dogs, but everyday movements are not the same as feeling movements. Before SIT 2, I had no idea my feelings

79

had movement and sound. The more I allow myself to genuinely feel, the more instinctually guided I am during my SITs and in everything I do.

A tip if you're overthinking your SIT would be to pause for a moment. Close your eyes, take some deep breaths. Remind yourself there's not a morally correct or spiritually evolved right way to SIT. There's *only* an honest one. Then let all sounds in. When you let all sounds in, without placing conditions or judgments on them, it gives you access to how you're truly feeling. The foundation of SIT 2 is to find and then know, accept, and unconditionally love the feelings through. This process reintegrates our feelings back in. They are no longer foreign (outside/AI) to us. Old conditioning and its reelality reels rise to the surface and is cleansed by reality. Therefore, old conditioning is replaced with light (*knowing*/self-acceptance that instils new information and understandings).

Remember this: The moment you tell yourself you should act a certain way and be someone you're not, you've fallen "asleep" in reelality and bolster old conditioning.

When I am aware, and therefore instinctually guided to *SIT* still, I understand that movement can be a distraction that removes me from accessing my emotions. For example, I've asked the yoga participants in my class when they're in longer held poses "Are you moving to go deeper into the uncomfortable or are you using movement as a distraction to try and get away from it?"

This does not mean I won't engage in movement later. So long as I have a genuine willingness to enter a SIT, I trust I'll be shown the way. You might be thinking "but isn't trying to be still activating a condition?" To which I would encourage you to repeat asking yourself the question, "Are you moving to go deeper into the uncomfortable or are you using movement as a distraction to try and get away from it?" The more we unconditionally feel, the more we *know* ourselves and what to do (move or remain still).

We start recognizing more when we're being manipulated by our old conditioning and are therefore being conditional during our SITs and can snap ourselves out of it sooner. This also helps us to live more unconditionally in our daily lives.

There will be times during your SITs where you will feel peaceful and other times where you will feel uncomfortable. Keep in mind, it is often in the uncomfortable, that we find our greatest self-realizations and transformations.

What was it that Tom Hanks character in *Forest Gump* famously said? "Life is like a box of chocolates; you never know what you're going to get."

The more times we choose to reflect, the less scared we are to feel. Some of us (myself included), when faced with a dilemma, look forward to opening the box because we know from experience that what's inside is there to ultimately help us feel better.

Unconditionally Accepting Feelings, Judgments and Conditions

An example of a condition would be setting an alarm on your phone to put a time limit on your session. If you truly want to make time for yourself, turn your phone off.

An example of a judgement would be telling yourself "I am wrong for having these feelings," or "I should not be acting this way. Or "the sounds I'm making sound ridiculous," or "the movements I'm making look ridiculous, so I'm not going to make any sound or movement unless it comes out the way I think it should."

Let the feeling exhaust you. You'll know you have unconditionally accepted the feeling because when it's over, you'll be mentally and physically calm and relaxed. For example, I might enter a SIT physically tense and emotionally frustrated but because I allowed myself to fully feel and embody being frustrated. The resistance I initially felt is no longer in charge of me. "It" has been burned out and deactivated by my willingness to fully accept it as it is. Because of this, I feel peaceful.

At this stage, if you haven't already, you may be witnessing other time zones to which you will not just be watching but actively be a part of. For example, if the image you see yourself in is you as a child, you'll experience the feelings you felt back then in the present. If this is the case, don't try to act like an adult. Allow yourself to be the child.

Allow yourself to sink in and take hold of whatever time zone and feelings come up. Remember, your point of power always resides in this time zone. When you accept how you felt back then in the present, you change your timeline. Be supportive and loving with your feelings as they move. See them for the gift that they truly are. When we unwrap with absolute acceptance, it blows the box on our shoulders wide open.

I've found that for me to be unconditional means I must see my way through being conditional. I cannot be in love with anyone until I accept *all* of myself. When I thought I could, it was because I was being operated by the ghost, asleep to the conditional world.

Listen up! This next part is important. Let's say the emotion you're faced with is rage or any other emotion you find heated. To unconditionally accept any emotion doesn't require you to love it. If you feel rage or fear, that's okay. Whatever the emotion is, feel it just as it is (which is complete until you try to make it something it's not). That's how rage transforms into love.

Don't say to yourself, "I have to love my rage to set myself free of it." Rage doesn't transform into love by trying to love rage—that only adds fuel to the fire. Not only that, but it makes you more ignorant to rage, which makes you less willing to accept it. This also means you can't know love because you're stuck in your ignorance and are not accepting rage in its completeness.

Closing

If you've reached step four successfully that means you have fully allowed yourself to feel your emotions without restraint and have therefore seen your way through them. In step four you have deactivated the charge surrounding the feeling and from the past feelings controlling you in the present. At this stage, we understand embracing how we feel rather than fighting it puts us in charge of our own timeline. No one out there decides our lives for us.

After the storm, sounds are quieter and fuller at the same time. The room somehow becomes more alive and breathing with me. At this stage I sometimes thank my feelings in a variety of different ways. But there are also times when I don't and instead bask in the fullness of nothing and everything all at once. In other words, I allow things to unfold naturally. We don't want to overthink this moment because it can overthrow it. Let yourself be as you are with no pressure to do anything but be. The choice will be based off how you feel in that moment. Honor it, whatever it is.

I also want to say that the process of feeling is not always going to be an easy road—especially in the beginning. Remember, Soul came here because it wants to do the work. It wants to experience contrast. So just because we do a couple SITs doesn't mean we're going to feel better right away. Our brain requires time to reroute itself. You're carving out new trains of thought, new ways of being that can greatly benefit your overall wellbeing and in the early stages, that can feel very unfamiliar and make you want to give up.

If you feel like your life is going nowhere or feel purposeless and stuck in someway, remember what's happening behind the scenes. Emotions are coming to a head on purpose because they're ready to be transformed as a means to create purpose. The creator within is asking you to move old conditioning so that you can be creative. When we create, we generate life, which makes us feel purposeful. When we get out of our astral heads we connect to our physical bodies and become one light vectors, generators, creators, life makers, and livers.

Discovering SIT 2

SIT 2 arrived six months after losing the love of my life—Abby, my five-pound Yorkshire Terrier. After her passing I endured nine straight months of day and night panic attacks. Before that, I only thought I knew what pain was. Some people have human children while others have furry ones. Abby was like a daughter to me. My heart had never been filled with such joy, love, and pain all at the same time. To help you understand the SIT method part two better, I am going to share one of my experiences with you.

After Abby's passing, I couldn't sleep. I was waking up every hour most nights for several months until I decided to SIT. One night around three a.m., I woke up feeling the same way I always did: frustrated, defeated, and exhausted. The perfect excuse to why I told myself I couldn't SIT and yet in the same token, it was the perfect reason to SIT. When we feel exhausted and are at our wits ends, we're closer to the feeling than we would be if we were not. We are more vulnerable and open, which is why I felt so overwhelmed and defeated. The feelings were rising to the surface like a zit ready to be popped.

After several minutes of arguing why I was too tired to SIT, something in me decided to put pen to paper. I began writing down how I felt. "I am so tired of being tired, I'm beyond angry and that makes me feel powerless which makes me feel even more pissed off! I hate feeling tired. I hate feeling exhausted, I hate not sleeping, I hate missing Abby, I hate my life right now. I can't handle it anymore and I want to throw a fit over it but I'm too exhausted!" The words kept reeling out of me (something I later realized was me using the story as ammunition to access the feeling). I asked myself what does this fit sound like? "I don't know," I whined. A couple seconds later, I forced a pretend baby whine out. Within seconds, this led to clenching fists and eventually to more authentic wailing sounds.

Within a matter of minutes, I was crying so hard that after a short while I felt an immense pain in my jaw.

I began to cry even harder. "Fuck it. I don't care if my jaw snaps in half. Fuck you jaw! Fuck you for thinking you can control me!" I knew that if I held back the intensity of the sound leaving my body and the impact it was having on my jaw, I'd be placing a condition on it. Therefore, I wouldn't be fully accepting it just as it was and needed to be. I'm not suggesting that if your feeling physical pain during your SIT, that you should experience it. I'm simply sharing what took place for me. The tears were now pouring out of my eyes with such intensity that they felt as though they were leaping horizontally from me.

Suddenly, I was in the crib. I'm assuming somewhere over the age of one but under the age of three, because I was standing up screaming bloody murder while holding onto the bars. "No one hears me. Where is everyone? No one cares about me, again. Where is everyone? Can anybody hear me? Please pick me up! No one wants to pick me up. I must be disgusting." These were some of the things I remember thinking while in the crib. My skin began to ache, and I suddenly realized I was cold and shaking now on my side in the fetal position, rocking myself in the crib. "I'm so cold. Please help me it hurts."

When we SIT, we energize the past into our present. Unconditionally accepting the feeling ends up collapsing time. When I allowed the feeling to take me, my brain opened a door that, prior to that moment, had been locked from my conscious awareness. I later realized my skin hurting in the crib was linked to my skin hurting each night I got into bed after Abby passed. Because I was unaware of its origin, it was now being triggered as a means to process it. Back then I was unable to digest what was happening because I was too young to understand it. But here I was, emotionally in 1979 or somewhere close to that, ready to see the memory and its trapped emotions through. In that moment I was experiencing two time zones at once as time occurred simultaneously.

The memory of me as the baby surfaced and I could not only hear my baby thoughts I also allowed myself to cry as the baby. I didn't try to change a thing about where I was or overanalyze the situation with my adult brain or say, "That's enough." I didn't look at the time or stop to journal it. In that moment I was the baby, and she was in my adult self. All our feelings happening together and no time barrier blocking us. We cried together for some time, maybe 20 minutes. I can't be sure.

I became aware of my adult body on the couch the same time I realized I was in the fetal position rocking myself. The pool of tears around my eyes felt warm but I was no longer crying. My body and mind felt calm, and that's when I knew the feeling had been exhausted, unconditionally accepted, transformed, and reintegrated. I was at peace.

When time happens simultaneously and we are a part of it, time has no boundaries. Therefore, we are timeless. When we allow the past to wash through us today, we "sea" and in that vast ocean it no longer challenges us. When we give the wounded child our full attention, by lovingly listening, they no longer feel abandoned by us. They no longer need to get our attention by throwing a fit that would take us over and filter our lens today. Instead, because we have exposed the program, it no longer hides and controls us. We can then see today clearly, and when we feel, the act is over.

In the beginning when Abby first passed, I screamed and yelled and moaned like I had never known I could. The feelings coming out of me were guttural and primal—shocking even. I was feeling and expressing emotion but not to the point of exhaustion because SIT part two hadn't arrived yet. I would emotionally come undone to a point, and then stop. I was conditional with my feelings. "Okay you've been crying forever, now it's time to stop it." Or I'd scream at the top of my lungs for several minutes until it felt like I might bust a vein in my throat and then say, "Okay *now* that's enough. Get it together. Take some deep breaths in and out and try to focus on the good times with Abby and the love she brought to my life." Everyday I'd unknowingly put conditions on my feelings that would add to the overwhelming belief that I couldn't survive without her by my side.

The interesting thing about this SIT (and so many others for that matter) was that I wasn't thinking I was going into it with the intent to resolve something from so long ago. In the crib I met with emotions that were tied to me feeling abandoned, rejected, and disgusting. Emotions that made my skin hurt later when it was over. Because the word disgusting was conditioned into my brain, it was later formed into an experience that was compounded (I'll share more about this in the last chapter). I realized these emotions were also tied to the loss of Abby (I was so emotionally sensitive, I had to wear long sleeve pajamas to bed because the sheets touching my skin hurt after Abby passed). This is a prime example of how and why it's important that we never question the feelings rising or try to change them. Their taking us to a place that requires feeling for healing to occur.

What's important to keep in mind, though, is that to change the past requires total acceptance of how we feel today. In doing so, we may or may not be flooded with a memory. So, if a memory doesn't surface when you SIT, remain confident in the feeling. We don't need the memory to repair or heal pain today. All that is required is the feeling from the memory. Without feeling, we remain prisoners to the past.

Immerse Yourself in the Feeling

I believe that God (our projected whole and absolute self) gives us what we need to heal and repair our fragmented thinking. He (representing a universal term for the glue or living being inside all of us that's energetically binding us to one another) brings back to us that which we are remaining ignorant to or the things requiring our attention. What we think we want and are even praying for is often what we are resisting emotionally in ourselves. This is why we sometimes feel like our prayers aren't being heard or that we aren't getting what we asked for. When we understand Soul purpose, we also understand that what's coming our way is the opportunity to accept something within ourselves that was once overlooked. Behind the screen, everything that comes our way is for us. Anything outside of that is being driven by the ghost and is how we see life as something that is happening *to* us (victim mentality) instead of for us.

Feelings are the magnetic polarity of the Soul. It is our feelings that invite our experiences. When we don't accept our feelings, we attract electrically run situations into our lives that stress us out of our bodies, making us believe that our purpose is out there when in reality it's in the inside out. In other words, it's in the inside first then it becomes the outside.

When we accept how we're feeling today, we align to situations that are overflowing with wellness in all areas of our lives, not just some or none. *Know* that you are not alone, even if right now you feel like you are. We are eight billion minds vibrating together.

Without the panic attacks, I would have continued running. The panic inspired me to "sea" myself. I'm not saying I'm cured from anxiety, worry, or stress, because I'm not. But I'm also not controlled by them in the same way I once was. However, I won't really know how I feel until the next trigger or inspiration arises. I'm not a fortune teller, nor do I want to be one. I am, however, someone who understands the difference between reality and reelality. Because of that, I am no longer someone who runs from their feelings and is therefore operated by them.

I am freer than I once was. What I was unaware of back then that I am aware of now is that the panic attacks were the release of a lot of old conditioning. Losing Abby inspired me to feel all of that at once, repeatedly for nearly a year. When I would have a panic attack, I would literally believe I was going to die, and that's because parts of me were dying. The panic attacks were many layers of denied and unaccepted hurt from my past—surfacing on purpose to create purpose. I would no longer be controlled by an unaccepted and unloved past, and could be more present and loving with myself and others today.

Knowing that I might never get through all my hurt used to terrify me. But because of the tools I've acquired, I understand that the more I run from how I feel the more I hurt in the long run. Time always catches up with us when we're being run by it. I understand that ignoring my Soul purpose here in this physical body makes me feel purposeless out there.

Remember, it's never our feelings that hold us back—it's our resistance to feel that does. Since our feelings reside in the physical body, which is always in reality, when we accept how we feel we become a part of reality. There is no longer suffering on a negative belief in *outer space*.

It is my belief that Abby came into my life to show me unconditional love so that I could feel and know my way through the terror of believing my mom never loved me, when in truth, she did. When Abby was

89

alive, she brought so much joy to my life that it hurt because in my mind, love hurt.

It did not matter what I told myself about love as an adult because it was what my brain recorded when I was a young child that operated me. Back then, I didn't understand what I was feeling or what to do with those feelings. I believe my brain naturally tucked the pain away for me as a way to protect my body from experiencing a stress overload. Then, later in life, when I was more prepared to handle those emotions, my brain would bring them forward via the trigger of Abby's passing for me to "sea" my way through.

When I was a child, I was unable to process those feelings, and as the years passed by so did the layers of my denial towards love, bolstering my fear of love. Before SIT 2 I thought I'd mended the relationship with my mom even though I didn't. There was still a massive amount of emotional scaring there that was still dictating my life. It wasn't until I was forced to feel it during the SIT that I became aware it was still there. But that is the thing I most look forward to now. I never know where my SITs are going to take me. What used to scare me (unknown/present moment) no longer makes me shake. If anything, because I have accepted more parts of myself, I'm able to trust the wobble as something that's there to serve me. While I am amidst the wobble, I feel steady and centered. Remember, the ghost is manipulative—it will lead us to believe that because we've intellectually moved through something we've emotionally processed it when we haven't. Denial is like a black hole that continually sucks in surrounding energies. Even light can't escape it. Therefore, denial blocks understanding.

The thought I was terrified to lose Abby was a conditional thought. It overrode my ability to unconditionally love her. This is what many of us do when we fall in love. We conditionally love because we are attached to the fear of losing it. Ask yourself, have you ever been in love with someone but feared losing them, whether a spouse, child, family member? If so, you'll understand what I'm saying.

If I were loving Abby unconditionally, it wouldn't have hurt. I was just telling myself I loved her to try and cover up the terror I felt over it. Real love doesn't hurt, and when we say it does it's because we're out of our mind.

To see my way through the fear of love meant that I had to lose it. I have found that death has many facets and one of those facets for me, is terror. "Sitting" with terror was the most intense, scary, and powerful SIT so far. It pushed me to my limit and then miles past it, to the point where for a moment, I thought I might never come back from it. I mentioned how water, when we are submersed in it, can assist in heightening consciousness, enabling us to hear our uncluttered self. When I decided to SIT in terror, I did it in the bathtub. I am not going to go into the details about it here but will say it was the most powerful SIT so far.

Our spouses, families, co-workers, friends, and strangers are all going to trigger us. When we seize the opportunity to evolve from it, we set ourselves and those around us free. When we don't, we remain ignorant and stay at war. The reason why relationships end is because one person, or both, aren't willing to face themselves through one another. If you are blaming someone for not giving you what you want like I did time and time again in my past, it's because you're acting like a child but not being the child. Until you SIT in a real temper tantrum and *See It Through*, the wounded child conditioning will continue to operate you.

Some of you may be thinking that you have nothing to feel or nothing to work out. But ask yourself why you think that is. A friend of mine once said he doesn't think about anything painful because he's practiced and gotten good at not thinking about anything emotionally painful.

"Why would you want to think about that kind of stuff when you don't have to?" he said.

For me, not wanting to accept all of myself is what led me to drink myself into oblivion night after night. It's also what gave me high levels of anxiety. The more I tried not to feel, the more I dug myself six feet under.

Today I understand that for me to be free, I must notice and feel everything. I cannot busy myself with distractions or come up with excuses that will deter me from honoring that path.

For me, the more I SIT, the less judgmental and conditional I am with myself and that makes me less judgemental and conditional with others. Accepting how I feel allows me to be more empathetic with myself and others. When I clean up my own mess, I don't have anything to dump onto those around me. I now understand that when I say I can't really judge anyone because they are me and I haven't seen my way through the feelings rising in the judgment, I bolster pretending not be judgmental. This does not set me free of judgment. Instead, it adds a thicker layer over top of it for me to feel controlled by. When I don't allow myself to use the judgement as ammunition to access the feeling, I am being run. I give my power over to the ignorant belief and program called "I don't judge others because they are me," when in truth, I do judge them. Today, I take advantage of the judging part because it shows me the feelings I've been running from, which helps me not to be run. When I don't, my real feelings stay hidden, and my programming runs me. The more I pretend the more I am affected by fake lights and fake people (something I explain more in the next chapter). This only adds to a lack of oxygen, which leads to inflammation. Since it's my belief that all inflammation is emotional first and becomes physical, I not only have inflamed thinking, but I also have inflammation in my body. The more I reinforce this kind of thinking, the more it can turn into something beyond my ability to repair it.

SIT Method Part Two

The more authentic I am during a SIT, the quieter and less argumentative my head is later. SIT 2 is a process that allows you to get to know your feelings/emotional body. It's about immersing yourself into the feeling to the point where the feeling feels safe to speak its story to and through you. So many of us have no clue how we really feel because we are too wrapped up in the charged story. This process is about you allowing and accepting parts of yourself that you've created and then denied and abandoned. These are the parts of yourself that you now have the opportunity to hold, be there for, listen to, understand, and ultimately, unconditionally love.

Chapter 7

CO-CREATING REALITY

When we are in reelality, we forget who we are. We don't remember our inner connection, which is why we see ourselves as separate and create walls that intentionally divide us from one another.

For example, a phrase like, "I'm not religious, I'm spiritual," is something I heard often while working in the yoga industry. No matter how the ghost tries to politely and, therefore, spiritually put it, being spiritual is a religion because it seeks to be separate from other types of spiritual thinkers.

This headspace in reelality is driven by the automatic mind when conscious thought and action is removed. When active in our subconscious mind, we are hypnotized by a learned behaviour rather than an instinctual one. We are a repeater of someone else's information. When a learned behaviour is activated, we become hypnotized by the script.

For instance, a person in program mode hovers in reelality with their conscious mostly turned off. I say mostly because for one to be unconscious there must be a degree of consciousness to control the unconscious part. This explains the outside world.

When the subconscious is running, not only are we a repeater of our ancestral script, but we also become repeaters of other people's scripts. For example, what we learn in school is not ours, it's someone else's. We study and memorize someone else's knowledge and experiences and then put it up on our walls (framed degrees) and call it ours. New information comes from old conditioning going out. In its place, new understandings fill in, which is what new information is. Ask yourself *what do I know* versus *what have I been taught to know.*

Let's take Einstein's theory of relativity. Einstein theorized that time does not flow in only one direction, that the future exists simultaneously with the past. In reelality, we don't "sea" the projection and, therefore, cannot feel the inner connection. Consequently, we believe we need direction. When we feed into our stressful stories, it's easy to forget where our point of power lies. When we have no power, we're no longer capable of self-direction. This emotionally splits us in half, giving us two directions that are inescapably linked together. This, in turn, brings on confusion and no self-direction.

The knowledge that time is linear limits your growth and understanding. You believe it because it is what you've been taught and regurgitated over and over again in your life. When you understand that time is relative, you open yourself up to new self-awareness about yourself and your direction or purpose.

The past, future, and present are concepts of time that control us only when we are in reelality. Reality is not controlled by time. It is instead time-less, which means it's in a constant state of beginning without a middle or end.

When we haven't accepted a negative feeling from our past, it determines who we are today. We bring *it* into the *now* (which is a weigh station in between the conflicted past and future built by the astral and spirit mind) and make the present and future toxic. We can't have a bright future when it's being driven by a negative past (because the two are bonded together by the *now*). Until we look at what is happening now and *See It Through*, we can't be present. This also means our physical bodies can't repair and we age rapidly and poorly. When we *See It Through* time ceases to exist and we live the present moment with the endless beginning (the EB).

Many of us fear time because we're not sure of what's waiting behind the end point. We think it's not up to us. Another word for time could be God, and another word for God could be religion, and another word for religion could be control. This statement is not meant to imply there is no God, but only that when we turn on the need to be saved by anything we become enslaved by it.

When we make any word bigger than ourselves (like fearing the idea of death because we don't know what comes next), we inescapably make it absolute. For example, the word God might feel overwhelming if you have an issue with God and would rather say words like universe or source in its place. Hearing the words dad or mom could also be overwhelming or painful to someone with unresolved parental history. Basically, when a word or group of words feel painful, they become bigger than us. A simple word or phrase can control how we think and feel.

In doing so we end up turning the thing, deity, or person on and ourselves off. This gives the outer all the power and us little to no power. Make time absolute and it decides your expiration date. Time now can remove your power just as God has the power to take heaven away from you.

I know for me, growing up I never used the term God because of my mom's own unresolved past. The word God meant something religious, and since religion was frowned upon in our home, it wasn't a word I naturally aligned with. The word was further compounded when I got into yoga. The common theme proudly said by nearly everyone around me was

"I'm not religious, I'm spiritual. I use words like universe or source energy to describe God."

Until I *sat* with the word God, it had power over me. Not seeing the word through encouraged the electrical charge to take energy from me. Today, I feel aligned enough to use the word God. If it triggers you to read the word here, instead of reinforcing its power over you, go in and explore it. In doing so, you embody real power and expand you're state of consciousness as well your overall wellbeing. As opposed to reel power that makes you think, not saying certain words means you've got rein over them.

If you have an aversion toward any word, try *sitting* with it so that it no longer controls you. You may come out the other end quite surprised at what you find.

When we act conditionally, we move out of reality and into reelality where we no longer project an all-encompassing source of love but a conditional one instead. We are the only ones who decide whether we will spend eternity in bliss or burning in hell.

As humans, we have been taught that we only have so much time and are at its mercy. If, however, we had been educated to see time as a mechanical mechanism to aid us in scheduling certain applications that simplify our daily routines, we might not see it as linear or feel so frustrated by it.

Timelessness is unconditional, which is why so many of us do not understand it. There are no strings attached, and so it isn't dominated by cause-and-effect repercussions. Timelessness is the beginning that never ends. It is reality, and when we are there, it's friendly. The endless beginning stands still and is in motion throughout life at the same time. It's a constant unfolding of now and what keeps our bodies alive when we continue thinking. It is not controlled by cause and effect and cannot be pulled in two directions. When we trust where we are, there's no more past or future to feel controlled by. We are no longer in need of a God to save us from hell. We are standing still amidst the motion of our existence.

Throne vs. Thrown

Many of us can relate to the five outer senses: touch, taste, smell, hearing, and seeing. The sixth sense, or intuition, is not considered real by some but is instead more of an extrasensory perception beyond the acknowledged five. Intuition to the ghost is what instinct is to the mind. It sits at the core of its being. The difference between the two is that intuition thinks or guesses, and instinct knows or trusts.

Intuition reads time only, which is how and why psychics connect to it and disclose our future. When in the astral realm, we align naturally to other floating heads. But when we're connected to our physical bodies and are grounded, there's no need to ask what is ahead. We are fulfilled right now.

When we are not mentally grounded in our physical bodies, we're not seated in our throne. Throne representing physical body, our mind has thrown itself out into reelality. This makes the mind ignorant and arrogant, which is how it makes some people royal, chosen, or accepted and others not (peasants or unaccepted). The external world is the *thrown* subconscious mind I call ghost that some of us are aware of being in and some are not. When we are unaware that the outer environment is thrown from within, it's because we're not taking responsibility for our perception, and it controls us.

Ghost hovers in the thrown above its throne, looking down its nose at the people below it. On the other hand, when it is grounded in its physical body, the mind sees everyone as its equal. Therefore, everyone is royal. Ghost believes abundance manifests via hard work, and the golden exception is that family hand me downs (trusts) don't count. The mind is the opposite. It understands that regardless of silver spoons and individual uniqueness, we are all royal. The mind's life feels mostly effortless. I say mostly because no matter which end of the battery we lean toward most, we still have both sides in us.

The ghost's realm involves spirits. This is not to be mistaken for Soul, as spirits are broken off parts of the Soul that have gone astral and grown their own identities. For some, the more spiritual they become, the more judgemental they are, only hanging around with a certain quality of people who are mindful, chosen, royal people that don't trigger them to feel unwell. Heaven forbid you get triggered and feel pressured to repair or heal your broken thinking. If you're being mindful, it's because your mind is full and needs emptying. To do that, many of us just need to spend time with family. For many of us, family can make us feel crazier than our everyday fluffy friends can. Fluffy friends tell us what we want to hear but not want we need to hear to heal.

If you want to unconditionally accept *all* of yourself, hanging around with people that make you face who you're trying not to be are the ones that enable us to see our pain through. I call these people Soul mates because when you're ready to "sea" it, they're the ones that help you understand love.

Energy Centers in the Body

Some of us have been conditioned to believe that what we are unable to see with our physical eyes, is more holy, like God and angels. Chakras fall into the same category (chakras representing energy centers in the body). Therefore, there is a tendency to believe that what we can't see is more evolved.

For example, spiritual practices such as meditation, unblocking or balancing chakras, astral travelling, etc. can, for some, lead us to think we are in a higher vibrational place than those around us.

Co-Creating Reality

When we become attached to thinking what we can't see has more power, we lose sight of the tangible reality. We become less grounded in the physical body. This makes us teeter totter in reelality, and we wobble *out there*. This throws us off center and away from our physical bodies. Remember, the more out there our thinking goes, the bigger the electrical gap between mind and body, and you and I is.

In every yoga instructor training I've taken (along with a few other modalities), I've noticed that the common thread between them is fear. For example, some of the facilitators taught us the importance of protecting ourselves from other people's energy. I want to address things like burning sage to energetically cleanse ourselves or envisioning white light around us, because what this does is it instils fear.

The more we see our struggles through, the less we project onto others. The less we project, the more we reflect and can see that what is pointed directly at us has come from us as a means to inspire the release of an emotion that requires feeling for healing. When we *See It Through*, we deactivate the charge (which remember is the story) that is preventing the two of us from being together.

Now I don't *need* to protect myself from you. I understand that when anything in my life feels like it's coming to a head or coming at me, it's because I'm ready to move through it. I'm no longer needing to overlook excuses that will keep *it* awake and me asleep. If I've cleansed anything, it's my thinking. When I SIT, the mother and father (or ghost and mind) within me join hands and become one. Because of that, I'm no longer teeter tottering to one side of my two halves (masculine and feminine), creating a wobble or division within myself. I am centered within my Soul and because of it, I'm also centered in the collective Soul. There is no longer an argument standing between you and I. I am with you without having to be physically next to you.

When you believe that you need to protect, clean, clear, or purify your energy field from others, it's because you're in fear, not love. This makes you want to blame them for the way you're feeling. You are in your astral body not your reality body. That's essentially what we do if we haven't resolved our parent (mother/father) or God issues. We project them onto those around us. For example, until I genuinely felt at peace in the relationship with my mother, I believed I had to protect myself from women. Since defense is an attack, I attracted hurt women that confirmed and reinforced my feelings of being hurt and abandoned by her. This would then give me the perfect excuse to resent them, be angry at them, and blame them for it so that I could make them wrong and me right. Little did I know at the time that all that mindset did was take power (love) away from me.

If you are someone who considerers themselves knowledgeable on chakras, see if for a moment you can remain open to hearing a new perspective. Keep in mind that I'm not asking you to change your mind about anything you already know. I'm simply asking that you remain open to the possibility of learning something new. Pay attention to how it feels in your gut brain rather than your thinking brain. Feel it out rather than trying to think it out. Remember, new information can't enter when we're stuffed to the brim with old conditioning and think we know everything.

I'm now going to share a scale of where I believe the seven main chakras reside in the physical body and how they function. I will also explain chakra needs. How did this information come to me? The same way all new information does—by getting rid of old conditioning.

The more we resolve the pain from our past, the more we hear the self that connects to all selves. The one that does not need to fight, defend, or justify what it has to say. Just because what I have to say may differ from what someone else says, it doesn't make me separate from them. If anything, it makes me more connected to them because I'm not dependant on their approval. Therefore, I can support what others have to say rather than argue. From where I'm standing, all opinions are royal and when they're not, I see them through.

The spiritual mind tends to focus more on the upper chakras. These are considered by some to be of a higher frequency and more spiritually evolved. The problem that arises from this is it cuts us off from the lower chakras, the ones keeping you grounded in your physical body where your feelings and human purpose reside. Not only that, but the more focused you are on the upper chakras, the more ignorant you are to the lower chakras. Since it is the lower chakras that establish bodily connection, we lose sight of reality. Remember, our physical body is always in reality, and our ghost body is in reelality. Since what we resist persists, our need to reach some sort of attainment (Enlightenment, Heaven, Bliss, Ananda etc.) becomes that much more driven. I'll explain *needs* more in a moment.

Chakra scale:

#7: Crown chakra (Violet)
Location: Top of the head
Physical association: Pituitary and hypothalamus
Needs: Connection to the divine
#6: Third eye chakra (Indigo)
Location: Forehead between the eyes
Physical association: Pineal
Needs: Intuition, sense of purpose
#5 Throat chakra (Blue)
Location: Throat
Physical association: Thyroid
Needs: Self-expression
#4 Heart chakra (Green)
Location: Center of chest (heart center)

Physical association: Thymus

Needs: Love, relationships, and self-acceptance

#3 Solar plexus chakra (Yellow)

Location: Upper abdomen

Physical association: Adrenal glands

Needs: Personal power and ability to channel

#2 Sacral chakra (Orange)

Location: Lower abdomen

Physical association: Pancreas

Needs: Sexuality and pleasure

#1 Root chakra (Red) = Mistrust/ lack of self-acceptance =
     semiconscious = reelality

Location: Base of spine in tailbone area

Physical association: Gonads

Needs: Career, money mindset, and sense of belonging and feelings

Ground zero (White) Soul center = Trust/self-acceptance =
     consciousness = reality

Reelality is the backwards, upside-down version of reality. From the moment we fall from trust into mistrust, we feel forced upward as though we need to get somewhere. The ladder is the pyramid that pulls us into thinking we need to work hard to achieve greatness. Reality shows us how to work effortlessly, without need to climb, and no schemes to be exhausted by. Reality takes the effort out of the word work. We're still technically working but with minus the effort. Our job becomes more of an income routine we look forward to continuing. We move from hating our job to enjoying it.

I used to think that to get out of a low headspace meant I had to climb upwards to a better feeling thought of a higher vibration (upper chakras). I didn't realize the reason it made me feel more anxious was due to me pulling away from my physical body. Today, I understand this concept to be the other way around. For me to be happy requires me to surrender and drop into total acceptance of my feelings. That is where I break bottom and establish Soul center. When I SIT and fully allow the negatively charged belief to consume me, I no longer am in fear of it. This means *it* no longer has the power to hold me semiconscious.

Chakras act like vortices of energy. According to many spiritualists, these spinning vortices of energy should stay open and aligned to embody emotional and physical well-being. However, a closed chakra is not the problem that some people might believe, but instead are a result of those that are left open.

I believe since all chakras are open until we resolve our mental ignorance, they continue to act like drains that suck in similar surrounding energies. Not only do we attract back to us what we're emotionally putting out, but we also take in and take on similar energies (empath). When we've got too many feelers out there in other people's business and not our own, our bodies act like sponges absorbing other people's energies. The astral mind thinks it's connecting to those around it. In a way they are, but only because they're disconnected from themselves. When we accept *all* of ourselves, there's no need to take on other people's energy. All this does is hide, and not accept, how you really feel. Chakra wheels spin in reelality and when they are active, we feel confused, purposeless, and frustrated with our lives.

Chakras are multi-coloured lights made up of fragmented white light, all colours combined. As a one-light vector, we feel emotionally full. When our one light is shattered into pieces, it makes us feel as though we too are in pieces. Therefore, we need to look to people and places beyond us to be put back together again.

If you look at the chakras scale, you'll see that doubt resides at the root chakra. Doubt opens the root chakra program called *needs*, which then opens the other chakras needs programs. Now doubt is infused into all the other chakras and activates their astral needs. This is why so many of us feel overwhelmed by life and can feel like the weight of the world is on our shoulders.

For example, when the astral root chakra is active, its needs to revolve around career, money, and mindset for the sense of belonging, are more pronounced. Now, depending upon your perception of these things, you either need to have these things to be happy or you try to deny them. An example of denying these needs would be thinking that having financial success is bad or spiritually unevolved. The person refusing to need them might say, "I can't pay my bills but at least I'm spiritual." This is to say that overflowing wellness, which is what abundance is, is a bad thing. From there, doubt moves upwards into sexuality and pleasure.

Doubt in this area may make you wonder whether you're worthy of a certain amount of pleasure, if at all. When self-doubt or mistrust is infused into the second chakra it can create a slew of insecurities that make you feel powerless. Some will use sex to control, manipulate, or dominate to get what they want. Take a moment to look at the scale to see where you feel the most doubt and loss of power in your life right now. Also pay attention to any false sense of security, the part of you that thinks it's in control of certain areas of life when it's not. Ask yourself, are you in control of this part of your life or are you in fear of losing control of it? If its fear that's driving you, so are its *needs*.

The more we love ourselves the more we understand and experience unconditional love, which in turn also allows us to experience the extraordinary power of making love. This is a whole other topic, so I'm going to keep it short by saying, making love is the power of unconditional love moving through you. Making love is a condition less, duality, and polarity-free union that's spread out in the timeless and doesn't require physical touch with yourself or someone else.

Conditions live in the unresolved past (time). The ghost brings them forward to the present and pollutes it, rendering us reality blind. In turn it makes us love blind as well. The conditional mind needs rather than wants. Even so, it's important we seize the opportunity ghost is offering. When we unconditionally accept the fear-based emotions ghost gives us, a path to see our way through them opens up. In turn, we feel elevated and abundant. Without ghost, there's no contrast to understand and know its opposite.

We don't gain power from lack of self-acceptance. That makes us lose power, and since real power is unconditional love, when we feel a lack of everything, sex also becomes a conditional act. For us to know one another intimately, it means our clothes must come off.

Ask yourself if you *need* sex, food, alcohol, shopping, or even things like working out, or if you *want* these things. If you need something, you'll know where your head is at and what wheels it's turning. If you need something, it's time to *See It Through*.

Chakras drain our life force from our endocrine glands when our mind is *throw*n and in need of outer acceptance. Endocrine glands produce life much more than any measured lens can see. They are the life generators of our bodies. Without them, our bodies grow ill fast and die. Harmonious hormones flow from a harmonious mind that accepts *all* of itself, (the good, bad, ugly, and terrifying).

When we are centered and grounded in our throne, we don't need acceptance from others. Self-acceptance activates white light (all colors combined), while outer acceptance triggers broken white light (chakras). When our thinking is centered, the root chakra's needs are no longer pushing upward opening the other chakras. Therefore, we're not in need of any-thing, which means we attract overflowing wellness with little effort.

Since the root chakra floods all the other gates, the only way out is through the same way we got in: the root chakra. For us to wake up from the nightmare, we must break bottom. We do this by allowing ourselves to feel our feelings. Feeling our feelings makes us vulnerable, which is a form of falling. Therefore, when we SIT, our mind falls into, and then through, its feelings. For some, this fall happens when we hit rock bottom or have an epiphany like I did in the whiteout.

This can be a life-motivating experience so long as we hit bottom and break through it. Unfortunately, some of us get trapped at the bottom and don't break through, and our bodies die. I just happened to be one of the "lucky" ones (I don't believe in luck because to me it means preparedness) and even though I didn't put in what I would consider conscious work to get sober before the whiteout, there was still a part of me that wanted to get better. That part is what broke the bottom.

It also happens when we *See It Through* and have a moment of clarity like a SIT, or like letting all sounds in or rewriting your childhood have the potential to do.

Resolve the past and you will sober the thinking mind that needs and change it to a mind that knows because it trusts itself. This, however, does not mean that when we resolve an issue that energy moves upward like kundalini energy (a life force energy said to heal all mental and bodily ail-ments that resides at the base of the spine, asleep until it is activated and that I see as the body being in parasympathetic mode) supposedly does when it is awakened. In fact, it's the opposite. When the root chakra caves, it collapses the suspended energy being held in the other chakras above it and the energy moves downward to Soul Center, allowing the body to repair itself. The body is being drained of its minds programming. Repair your thinking and your body heals.

I also want to mention how we wear two kinds of crowns: a spirit crown (crown chakra) that wears us and a Soul crown that we wear. Spirits are astral and seek to conquer and divide. If we are being worn, it's because we're hypnotized by the ghosts self-absorbed thinking and have made some people royal and others not. When we wear a Soul crown, everyone else will be royal as well. There are no chosen ones. Soul has no walls, no partitions, no divide.

To expand on this topic, I've noticed throughout my life since the whiteout that every time I was about to have an epiphany or some sort of major shift in my life it was a crowning moment. When I was about to give birth to a new idea, it was because I was ready to let go of an old one. A crowning during birth is when the baby's head pushes through the opening of the vagina. In this case the crowning is representing a moment of clarity. I'm using this example to illustrate how giving birth to a new way of being can also be an equally painful and joyful experience. It can hurt to let go of the past but when we do, it doesn't wear us anymore.

The only way to release or transform a negatively charged belief is to unconditionally accept it. This is how we align ourselves to environments surrounded by crown wearers. Remember, when we see broken it's because our thinking is fragmented. When we are a one-light vector, we see everyone as royal.

Needs

The fear of not having our needs met is what energetically kicks us out of our physical bodies. When we "sea" our way through those needs fully, they collapse and no longer control us. For example, the more feelings I accept within myself the less I need others to love me. I now understand that when I don't see my mental chaos through, I need to be loved by everyone but me. So, to release needs I've got to go into the resistance of what it is I believe I need in that moment. For example, if I need my mother to love me, I get still and find the feeling behind the story. Then I write it down, as the first step in SIT 2 is to find the feeling.

When the past and the future are separated (mind conflicted/ghost), they are driven by the root chakra. Until we know we are in control of time, it and its wheels will control us. When we SIT and consciously bring the past into today and resolve it, we realize the past exists only when we think it into existence. Therefore, when we heal the past today, we make time happen simultaneously. Time collapses and with it goes everything we thought held value.

Wanting our needs fulfilled is not wrong, but there is not much light (self-acceptance) involved in it. Where there are conditions there's a lack of light and understanding. For example, in order for me to be happy, I need to make this amount of money, have this amount of sex, or travel this many times per year. Conditions bolster old conditioning.

Ask yourself, what do you spend most of your time in need of and how does it feel to need those things and not have them? Remember to ask yourself, *do I need this*, or *do I want this?*

If you need something, you give it power to own and hold you down, and this could be something as simple as a piece of furniture that you choose to move to a different residence. I need this piece of furniture because it was passed down to me through the family or because it was expensive, even though I don't really want it. Needing anything, be that material things or even people, can weigh us down and spin our wheels while encouraging negatively charged reels to control us.

When you notice the feeling need gives you, you'll have a better understanding of what a lack of light and understanding is. If you feel stressed or desperate, you'll know what resistance is. Resistance, remember, has very little movement. It sits in denial to how it really feels because it's captivated about how it thinks it needs to feel. Denial lives in reelality, not reality.

Where do you feel out of balance in your life right now? What areas do you feel most controlled by, or where do you feel the most out of control? The chakra scale can assist you in pinpointing these locations.

While we are here in physical bodies, we're all going to get triggered by people, places, and situations that stir up uncomfortable feelings. It's what we choose to do with those feelings that determines our overall wellbeing. The more accountable we are, the more connected to the whole we become. The more we trust (which remember must happen genuinely), the less spun we feel. We are either having a spiritual experience or a Soulful one. I am purposely repeating this because it strengthens our brains reflex to remember that we drift in and out of both to create purpose and to recognize the negative side of the battery (spirit) as being something beneficial. This is also necessary to the embodiment of the whole. Its harshness is there to aid us in knowing our whole self. Without fully understanding both sides, there's no power to awaken the battery body (Soul Center).

For us to *break bottom* (Soul Center), we must become vulnerable enough to trust the fall. Without it, we will constantly feel the need to climb our way to something that we think is beyond us. If we're exhausted by our thinking, our bodies will feel exhausted too. We will understand it's because we're being operated by spirit wheels. The longer we are in our astral body, the more frustrated and overwhelmed we become.

The scale of chakras shows us where we are. It's a barometer and when we're suffering, it will give us perspective. It will shed light on what in our body is being hit the hardest while under hypnosis. The chakra scale allows us to see more clearly where our physical bodies are being negatively impacted (inflamed). This makes us better equipped to want to repair our thinking. It also helps remind us of how in control we are, even when being worn. Observing the scale while under hypnosis helps to snap us out of it. When we look at the scale, it helps remind us to focus on the feeling rather than the story so that we can heal that part of our body.

Going into the emotion of it will help us remember our point of power, where we will truly have the free will to run our own lives.

When we *See It Through,* we are emotionally centered, and there's no more wobbling over a need for approval outside of us. Its foundation has been blown up and we're no longer living in a world where happiness is dependent on balance.

Pineal

If there's one chakra that's more popular than the others, I'd say it is the third eye chakra. It was the one most talked about in the yoga community where I worked, especially by those that practiced meditation. For a long time, I believed that with enough focused attention meditation could bring about enlightenment. Still, I have found trying to live life looking through my forehead (third eye) takes me further out, not in. Seeking mostly spiritual travel to other dimensions of mind gives me reality dementia. All the time spent in *outer space* makes me forget reality where my physical body resides. When we roam toward other dimensions, we experience *reelality* dementia, forgetting that our point of power is always here in the present. When we go astral, we're not in our physical vehicle or in our right mind.

To be clear, I'm not saying having mystical experiences like traveling to other levels of existence are negative. What I'm saying is when we believe these occurrences are taking place separate from or outside of us, we activate our astral body (*thrown*), making us a slave to the environment (*needing* the outer to feel fulfilled). For me to feel special or knowledgeable means I must leave reality where my physical body resides. When the pineal glands astral body called "third eye" is active, it throws our physical kingdom off center and creates hormonal imbalance (something I will explain further in a moment).

I find it odd that so many people attempt to stimulate the pineal (whether through meditation or yoga), as it receives blood flow second only to the kidneys.[1] The fact that there's already so much blood flow illustrates to me where many people already spend most of their time.

Not only do the two atmospheres (reality and reelality) produce their own kinds of oxygen, they also produce their own kinds of light: real light and reel light. Reality light is turned on only when its driver is functioning from an instinctual seat (throne). We are not in a state of self-doubt that would activate the thrown (blame the outer environment for the way we feel). This opens both our eyes ("sea"/panoramic view) and, in my opinion, instructs our pineal gland to produce optimal amounts of melatonin for our bodies. Melatonin regulates our wake and sleep cycles and is not just a hormone that the brain produces in response to darkness but is also a hormone of sunlight.

The more time spent in the *thrown* the more reel light dominates. Reel light activates the third eye chakra and is run primarily from a single-eye seat (a narrow perspective that only hears itself but not those around it). When this eye is turned on, we act fake not authentic. When we think it, we become it. What we put out comes back to us. Therefore, we become a magnet to all other imitation and fake lights near us—like blue light, for example. Blue light comes from electronics and can disrupt the circadian rhythm (sleep/wake state), negatively impacting the body's overall wellbeing. But don't take my word for it—pay attention to how it makes you feel. While the third eye, from my perspective, is pulling in outer fake lights in our daily lives, it's also by law (of the material plane) pulling in electromagnetic waves while we sleep. It is my belief that this gives us less overall melatonin (circulatory – pineal and subcellular—mitochondria), automatically creating chaos throughout our entire body.

When we are centred, we can still be under fake lights and among electro-magnetic waves but not be negatively impacted by them. For example, the reason we believe cell phones can hurt us is we don't believe they are extensions of us. Meaning when you live your life from Soul center or point of power, you understand you are the one powering your world and everything in it. When our body produces the proper amount of melatonin, we are not being zapped by electromagnetic waves and, therefore, wake up feeling bright-eyed and bushy-tailed ready to take on the day. This does not mean before we go to bed that we can fake talk our pineal into producing optimal amounts of melatonin. For our bodies to function optimally, we must first address what we avoid addressing.

The third eye is something that many of us transition in and out of daily. It is our God complex. This is why there's so much blood flow to the area, as it's where many of us already spend majority of our time.

When doubt is active in us and we're not in our physical bodies, our thinking is not grounded. This can make us question and overthink rather than know (trust) every detail of something. So, since the third eye is active only when we fall from trust into doubt, we fall into a conspiracy state of mind. The third-eye chakra, also called Ajna chakra, translates as "authority" or "command." When our third eye is on, it commands all our attention.

When our pineal gland produces reel light, we become self-centred. The room narrows and we suddenly think we know everything, and that the world revolves around us. There is no panoramic view for us to be able to connect with others. Instead, there's only a cramped, anaerobic, dark place that's difficult to exist in. Anytime we act conditionally, our third eye is speaking through us. This mode clips our wings, placing us in a cage. Reality light, however, supports an optic flow (panoramic view where we can "sea" and hear everyone's points of view), and this is where we are free to take flight.

When a stress-induced story takes over, it's only because we made it into an absolute in that moment. When we're not listening (Soul center/panoramic view), we are caught on, only hearing our own side of the story. This can lead us to repeat the same story reel, sometimes in multiple versions. For us to be accountable for our thoughts we must first realize we were the ones administering the "anesthesia" to ourselves. We choose to put ourselves under the influence of the ghost and be operated on. Many of us are unaware of this because it's what's most familiar in us.

Let me share a call I received from a friend as an example. Just remember to keep in mind that pretend light is reel light that produces stories that trigger emotions that can make us want to hide the real issue at hand. When the movie is playing, we only hear one side of the story and simply do not let ourselves see it any other way but pretend we do by using words like *yes* and *but*. After listening to my friend shame and blame her boyfriend for all the things he is not doing for her, I bring the narrative back to her by explaining this has nothing to do with him and everything to do with her. She deflects and says, "Yes, I know but . . ."

"Yes" and "but" together are not words that exist in reality's vocabulary. That combination falls out of a conflicted mind not open to hearing anything *but* themselves. Yes, but puts you in mathematics, and all that does is bring on more mathematics (multiply more stories like it). The same old storytelling never ends. If she truly did understand what I was saying, she wouldn't be making her boyfriend responsible for her happiness. When information is not *seen through*, it sits on the surface layer of our electrically charged shield, unable to penetrate a knowing.

Her call from that point on continues in the same direction as all her calls (nowhere, even if in her mind they absolutely go somewhere). She has made the story absolute and herself obsolete, which is why she feels like nothing and tells herself she needs her boyfriend to fulfill her. Her story then shifts into another, now supporting something else (caught on multiple reels).

"I told him that I won't tolerate certain things in his behaviour because that's how my ex treated me." Because she brought up her ex, she's no longer in one relationship but in two—with her past relationship and her current one. When asked if she could see this connection, her answer was still, "Yes, but . . ." All she can see and hear is her own opinion (third eye). This gives the story all the power and renders her to feel powerless. This is an example of how she's being controlled by multiple reels.

When we don't want to resolve a situation, it means we don't want to take responsibility for it (i.e., how we anesthetize ourselves). We hand the reins over to our programming to do the dirty work for us and are now oblivious to the repetition of the movie reeling out of us. We become the program (i.e., turning into an artificial intelligence).

Nothing on the outside gets resolved. Perhaps more importantly, nothing on the inside does either. No matter how much time I spent trying to lead her back, she wouldn't hear anything until she was ready to look inward. If we all took a moment to examine similar behaviour in our own lives, we would find a way to relate. I know I surely would.

When we're disconnected from our internal world, we feel vulnerable and victimized, which leads to laying blame on someone else for it. The more we avoid responsibility for our thinking, the more we reinforce our being hypnotized, leaving us comatose. We are unable to expose light (be the light), as the weight of our arrogance and ignorance and lack of accountability muddies the light in our cells, rendering us to feel dark and heavy.

If we are unable to be the light, we will not "sea" within ourselves nor in others. Our bodies will operate with an imitation light while drawing in more from the environment as well as from others' imitation pineal lights. Phony people attract, attack, and blame other phony people for their own phoniness.

We are either a one-light vector, a community of cells working together inside a Soul-body-mind, or a ghost body pointing the finger outward. In emotional harmony, we have healthy hormones. This is a widening of adroitness, which assesses the ability to regulate our behaviour to get what we want from others. It differs from psychopathy in that it's not intrinsically narcissistic or manipulative but refers rather to the set of social skills that allows one to work with others productively. This is reality co-creation. We are here to live our lives through one another, and until we wake up to "sea" that, we will remain prisoners of our thinking and hold others responsible for it.

Chapter 8

AFTER THE WHITEOUT

Let me say here that in no way do I have life figured out. I am still learning, growing, and at times being triggered by people and situations in my environment. I have had awakenings in my life, and I'm pleased to share some of them. Still, after experiencing them, I remain human enough to react to life. I am still affected by some things out there. I do get overwhelmed and taken down by large and small things like everybody else. The difference between the me of today and the me from the past is that I'm not nearly as lost and scared of life as I once was. I have come a long way! And I believe that is principally what we all want in life—to feel safe and purposeful most of the time. I'm happy to admit that is not something that happens overnight. If it did, we wouldn't have time to appreciate it.

One of the first things I remember after the whiteout is having a conversation with a man I started hanging out with a couple months before (the height of my addiction and lowest emotional point). I couldn't recall much about the time we spent together other than our first drink, which, to me, meant that I was being drugged to do God knows what with afterwards. I was so far gone at the time it simply didn't occur to me not to see him again—even after I woke up remembering nothing. Emotionally sick people find one another. I invited him over to tell him face to face that I no longer wanted to see him. He roared in my face and threatened to kill me. Six months later, five bullets were shot through my front windows, penetrating the walls of my kitchen, living room, and bedroom. Luckily, no one was hurt. To this day, the culprit or culprits were never found. That mattered less to me than knowing I was no longer a part of that scene, and it was no longer a part of me. Rather than clinging to a self-image from the past, as so many of us do, I was relieved to put it to rest and let it pass away. I let go of most of the friendships I had during that time and, in accordance with the law of cause and effect, they let go of me. Life pulls toward us that which we already are.

The First Year

During the first year after the whiteout, I felt drawn to things that I was never interested in before. For instance, I learned how to sit still in my body and meditate despite not having been taught how to practice. I would often sit for hours in a park, staring up at the sky and watching its complexity. Simultaneously, I felt swept away by all the little things because, for the first time in my life, I could see the vastness inside of them. Life had been triggered within me, and suddenly I was an active participant.

There were also more physical things taking place during that first year. One of them, it felt to me, was as though light were beaming out of my hands and the top of my head—something I later learned was the opposite for many energy workers. Instead of visualizing or feeling light leaving their body, they imagine light coming in. This is not to say that the way I sense the direction of light is the right or wrong way. I'm simply explaining my experience of it.

What I have to say next may extend into a lengthier conversation (perhaps in a future book), so for now I'll make what I have to say short. Today, when I work with light in relation to help assist those coming to me (clients) for any kind of energy expansion (be that relief from anxiety or any other emotional or physical blockage that's preventing them from living optimally), I do it by immersing myself and my projected self (the client) into the cellular memory of the whiteout. Then, in that immensity and for reasons still unknown to me, the person's negatively charged programs come to a halt (sort of like putting "it" on pause). Then, a lot of the time the client's body repair's and heals itself. Over time and depending upon the client's willingness to accept ALL of themselves, this can lead to permeance. I don't try to change my client's reality by trying to fix them. Instead I merge with them in the most loving vibration I have come to know thus far. When the blockage is out of the way, the person feels normal and sometimes they become aware of a larger sense of self. When the person is no longer being held captive by their negatively charged programs, they are not in a limited head space that would disagree with harmony and improvement.

That said, soon after the whiteout many of my female friends innocently teased me by suggesting I was a witch since none of us could explain what was happening. It seemed as though I was able to manifest and know things that normally would have been out of my reach. Before the whiteout, when I wanted something, there was work involved in attaining it. I never really thought about manifestation. It took the whiteout to widen my perception.

When I think back to that time during the whiteout, I recall not having emotional roadblocks at all. A thought entered my mind and instead of overthinking it and getting in my own way, I allowed myself to receive it. No question marks shielding me from it. What I found most satisfying though was that I never wanted anything I did not already have. As opposed to asking for expensive things, it was more about feeling emotionally full, being carefree, and having fun. Because I didn't feel tied-to or weighed down by anything, I felt an overflowing wellness of energy inside of me that sometimes just knew things.

For example, I would imagine a thunderstorm brewing (because I love the energy thunder generates) and minutes later there it was. I don't believe I was controlling the weather, but instead aligning to what was already in motion and simply foreseeing it. I didn't just imagine something happening—I believed it.

I continued to work in the bar, sober, for almost three more years after that. This fit perfectly into my new schedule, as I had a lot of free time during the day. There was plenty of time to spend in nature with my dog, time alone with myself (which I cherished), and plenty of enjoyable time with my friends.

Trusting In Dreams

During that same year, I started sleeping with a recorder next to my bed because of the lucid dreams I had. These dreams often included learning personal information about people I'd only had brief encounters with previously.

One of the first and most compelling events occurred when a man (let's call him John) I had seen before but never met approached me in the gym. He asked if I could get him and some of his friends into the bar where I worked. It was Stampede Week in Calgary, and the city overflowed with hundreds of thousands of tourists, many of them oil people. The bar was considered one of the more sought-after places during that week.

John said he had heard from a friend that I worked there. He was polite and attractive, and although he dressed in long sleeved shirts, it was obvious that he was in good shape. I took his phone number and told him I'd call if there were any issues. Otherwise, he could just expect to get in the next Friday night. He put his hand on my shoulder, thanked me, and said, "It was nice to finally meet you."

I finished my workout and went on with my day, not thinking more about the meeting until the wee hours of the next morning after having a dream with John in it. Since I didn't have to work in the bar that night, I ended up going to bed earlier than usual. At exactly three a.m., I sat straight up, grabbed my recorder, and documented the lucid dream I just had with John and his twin brother, whom I also had seen in the gym. The dream began with a young woman's face filling up my entire periphery. I had never before had a dream where one image dominated the scene. I knew the woman well, and at the time, she'd been struggling with alcohol and drug addiction to the point that I was concerned she might die.

The image of her face appeared for only a couple seconds before her skin began to melt and there was nothing but a skeleton. Out of her scull emerged a giant blue butterfly that overtook my vision. Then was gone. I stood in the lobby of my apartment with my Jack Russell terrier and one of my childhood friends standing next to me. The elevator doors in front of us opened and was full of people. My friend begged me not to enter, saying it was not safe, but I ignored his warning. The doors closed, and as it rose, everyone, including my dog, changed colours that ranged from red to orange to yellow. The numbers on the panel changed colours erratically too.

The elevator ascended a few floors and then violently dropped back down, creating a turbulent ride. The doors finally opened at the top of the building to reveal an outdoor patio bar, something that didn't exist in my waking state.

Gary, a more current friend, greeted me. I held up my cell phone to his face. Our every move was recorded like a movie, and I said, "Are you aware that you're in my lucid dream?"

"No," he replied.

I took his hand. "Come with me. I'll show you." I walked him to the edge of the building, which in my dream looked to be miles high.

I turned to face him, my back and feet at the edge, then let go of his hand and intentionally fell off. I fell at a surreal speed, thinking how hard it felt to breathe normally because of the wind beating along the sides of my face. I let myself plummet for several seconds before shouting, "Stop!" I immediately stalled and remained suspended in mid-air. I looked upwards, and in superhero position with my arms pointed overhead, I floated gracefully back up to the top, expecting to see Gary. Instead, there were two other people—John and his twin brother. But John was not standing upright. He was slouched and appeared drugged or drunk. John's twin brother held him in his arms.

Cam (John's brother) wasted no time introducing himself or briefing me on John's mental condition. He'd come to find me so that I might help with John, who had been performing surgeries, as he called them (self-inflicted mutilations), on himself for years. He went on to say that John had not been mentally well. This was according to the medical professionals, and at the moment he was at an emotionally dangerous tipping point. I expressed to Cam that I had no idea how I was meant to help John, but that I would figure it out.

"I can't imagine why this would be happening otherwise," I said. He thanked me, and I opened my eyes. I reached for my recorder and promptly began documenting details despite it being burned into my brain to this day.

A few hours later, I took my dog outside for a bathroom break. When we walked back into the building lobby reality seemed heightened in much the same way as it had in the dream. We stood in front of the elevator next to a woman, waiting for the doors to open.

Seconds later, a man nervously jumped out, shouting, "Don't get in that elevator. It almost killed me!"

To my own surprise, I enthusiastically replied, "Well then, that's my elevator," and hurried inside.

The doors closed to shocked faces. Seconds later, the elevator began to violently shake. As it ascended, I held the guard rails to avoid falling over. It rose a floor or two then dropped the same distance. It did this all the way up to the thirteenth floor where my apartment was. As it rose and fell, I laughed in disbelief as the scenario continued as if I were still in my dream.

"I'm making this happen. My dream wasn't just a dream. It was real, like this is real right now."

In that moment, I became conscious of the power of mind. I understood the capacity of self-trust and I knew, when I was in the dream, that I was in control and that it was not like any other dream. I was fully awake in it, as I was now. There was no difference between this moment and the dream. The only thing standing between the two is trusting that I am the one in control of my life—the one making it happen.

I called John the next day to tell him what happened. At first, he hung up, but when I called him back, he sat silently and listened. He was shocked and couldn't understand how I knew such personal details about his life. I later learned from him that only his immediate family knew of those things. John reluctantly (at first) decided to meet with me that evening.

Initially he seemed guarded, but after several minutes he seemed to relax. He asked how this happened, and I instinctually replied, "You're ready, John." I explained how our meeting in the gym the day before was not a coincidence, and that his Soul, or his conscious mind, paved the way for it to happen.

"I don't understand. I'm ready for what?"

"You're ready to move on from your past self, John. It has run its course, and now you're ready for a new course whether you realize it or not."

He had no idea what I was talking about but trusted what I told him only because of something I mentioned in the dream. When he was a child, he told his parents on several occasions that he saw a giant bat man but not the saviour Batman depicted in the movies. He reported seeing a man that was, in part, an actual bat. At first his parents wrote it off as a child with a wild imagination. But when he would not let up after several months, they became concerned. The final straw occurred when John's bedroom window was smashed in the middle of the night. He said that he was lying in his bed when the bat man appeared outside his window and stared at him like he wanted to hurt him. One minute John lay in his bed, and the next, he stood in the middle of a room filled with shattered glass.

After that night, his childhood disappeared. His parents had him committed to a hospital where he was diagnosed with schizophrenia and put on medication, which, he said, was what erased his childhood memories.

"My brother has always been the one speaking to others about our childhood for me because I can't remember it. So, when you said that I looked intoxicated like I was high in the dream and my brother was talking for me, it immediately grabbed my attention."

He showed me his self-inflicted scars (surgeries) from the past, along with his more recent, raw wounds. Over the course of a couple weeks, John and I had several phone conversations as well as a few in-person meetings where I mostly listened to him talk (one of the same things I do with clients today). I don't tell clients what I think they should do (which is a form of trying to fix them). Instead I listen to them, and because of that, I am able to communicate effectively. I coach and guide them through things they already *know* but have forgotten while caught in the filtered lens of their programming. In this sense, I act as a conduit.

Trusting Yourself and Attracting the Right Connections

A short time later, I instinctively was led to call a woman I did not know well but previously hired for a tarot-card reading. I confided the details to her, and, without hesitation, she agreed not only to help me but advised me to put a healing circle together for John. I followed her directions and called up several of my closest friends to join hands with me.

John was quite reluctant to attend and thought the whole thing sounded too out there for him. It took much convincing on my part to change his mind, but in the end, he agreed. When we arrived at the top of the hill, a 20-minute drive from my house but still in the inner city, we took our places and joined hands around him. Gene, the tarot card reader, instructed us all on where to sit and whom to sit next to. I positioned myself behind John with my hands on his shoulders and my legs extended out along the sides of his crossed legs.

Within seconds of the ceremony starting, I felt a surge of bright white and gold energy moving out of my body and into John (or it may have come out of him and into me, I cannot be sure). The surge was extreme enough that I thought my arms might burst open. The light moved at an incredibly fast speed, or at least that's how it felt.

Uncontrollable tears streamed down my face. These were tears of joy I had never experienced before, and they made me laugh out loud. My hands moved from John's shoulders to wrapping my arms around his midsection. This was unlike my experience in the whiteout, unique in itself, and served as something that, so far, I have had the great pleasure of experiencing only that one time.

When it was over, I hugged John tightly and said I believed our purpose together was now fulfilled. While I did not fully comprehend what that purpose might be, I innately knew it was complete. We spoke a few times after that, and each time he informed me that he felt more mentally stable. He was also no longer physically harming himself. Seventeen years later, he now has a wife, a child, and a successful career.

I do not suggest in the sharing of this experience that I healed John that day. I share this only to demonstrate how when we are in trust-with our-selves, we are in trust with the universe. When this happens the ability to connect with one another in ways that are beyond form can occur.

Post-whiteout, I was mostly self-absorbed. Before then, I had been running from myself, whereas afterward, all I could see was myself staring back at me through the reflection of every living thing. I loved what I saw and the ability to connect in the ways I did. If I were still in the same doubt-filled seat, I would have never been able to hear John and his brother. A healing comes only out of an innate knowing—a seat inside of you not chartered by a question that would stunt a healing's outward flow.

I didn't disbelieve or discredit anything about the dream or what took place afterward. Instead, I trusted where I was and that alone was enough for me. John may not have intentionally (at least to him) sought me out to have this experience with him, but something inside of him did—a flow of energy that reached beyond his physical container to both his brother (although his brother had no conscious memory of it) and to me. Without having to speak a word to anyone, John heard his own voice through his brother's and mine.

Chapter 9

MEDITATION PART ONE

What is meditation? If you Google how to meditate, one of the most common recommendations advises to focus attention solely on your breath, a mantra, or on an object like a candle flame. But I've found that if I focus on one thing, I'm using it as a distraction from all other things naturally wanting to occur with it. I'm in resistance to my environment and in an *outer-spaced* state of mind, leaving me open to astral travel (other dimensions or realms of existence). Give the ghost an inch and it will take you on a road trip you'll come to believe is more special than reality. If you're starting meditation with the intent of finding a more special place, all you will do is strengthen the desire to eventually seek out other special places.

When my yoga instructors taught me to focus only on my breath or mantra, this always made me feel worse. Trying to not think is like trying to kill yourself by holding your breath. Your body forces you to take a breath. In this same way, you can't stop your thoughts.

Reelality is governed by the laws of cause and effect. If you're meditating to try and stop something, you'll only make more of it—even if you've convinced yourself that you've mastered control. Sooner or later, the swell will rush in and you'll have to go back out to try again.

I mentioned the ghost measures its reality, making everything in it finite. When neurons fire in the brain they emit electromagnetic frequencies. Science captures those readings by using an electroencephalographic or EEG. Many people today gravitate to these kinds of measures only because they are in reelality (mistrust). Where there is lack there is doubt. This *outer* state of mind makes us need to be told of our whereabouts, our state of mind, and how we feel. Measurement is *on* time, whereas knowing (instinct) is *in* it (timeless). If I need to be told my state of mind, I am *out* of it (astral/ghost).

Love cannot be measured. If we need to measure our brain waves to find out whether we are in love, the answer is we are not in love, but instead are *on* it (surface level/conditional mind). Soul knows (trust), whereas the ghost thinks (doubt), which is why when the ghost is operative, we feel the need (first chakra) to attain proof that would then give us *knowing*. But that is not real knowing. Instead, it's reel knowing. Reel knowing is a slave to its environment. It needs the outer to confirm its happiness for it.

A friend recently told me she thinks she needs to get better at meditating to feel happier in her life. She is already in a power outage and now is giving even more power to something she already has tried hundreds of times but has never once made her happy. "How do you meditate, Jen?" My response: "By letting all sounds in." In a nutshell, when we don't allow the moment to unwrap itself in us, we wind it up more tightly.

The Act of Meditating

I meditate in two ways—with my eyes shut and with them open. When shut, they're still open to partaking in the experience of all things. I'm not trying to deny anything, and everything is able to manifest. I also meditate with my eyes open, which means that I take the time to self-care my way through that which makes me uncomfortable. I can walk around anywhere, whether a loud, crowded place or a quiet forest and still not miss my surroundings. I call this *walking meditation*. When I don't take the time to address what's bothering me, I end up bypassing it all. I call this *reelality walking me.*

I also want to discuss how I physically sit during a meditation. I almost always sit on the couch with my legs stretched out on an ottoman. The shape of a seated, cross-legged pose resembles a triangle, and from a triangle, some of us get mathematics (ghost mind). This is a mind not interested in experiencing the absoluteness of the moment. For me, one way to encourage an unwilling mind is to force myself to sit in a semi-comfortable or uncomfortable position. This does not mean I don't get uncomfortable sitting straight legged, because I do. But I'd rather sit as comfortable as possible to decrease my chances. When I'm not purposely forcing myself into a physically uncomfortable position, I'm more willing to experience discomfort in all areas, not just one. Also, when I allow discomfort to surface on its own time, I know it's because I'm ready (conscious or not) to move through it. Therefore, I'm not as eager to fight the position I'm in. I apply this way of thinking not just to my meditation but to all things in my life.

This does not mean I cannot sit cross-legged, but I no longer feel drawn to it. The more self-care I apply, the more instinctually guided I am to sit in the position that's going to best serve me that day.

There are times when I might also lie down to meditate, if only because I close my eyes to sleep at night. However, meditation, to me, means I am listening. So, often when I go to bed it's more of a spontaneous meditation. Relaxing my physical body while purposely paying attention to the sound of the room and the house, quiet or not, helps me to fall asleep peacefully. On the other hand, when I try to shut them down, I struggle and stay awake. Nevertheless, this technique does not make me fall asleep in my day meditations because my mind knows the difference between day and night. If it didn't, I not only would fall asleep sitting upright, but I'd also fall asleep during my walking meditations.

During COVID-19, there were months I didn't leave my couch for 10 to 12 hours a day, as I was deeply involved in ironing out my wrinkled thinking. I didn't force myself to be there—I wanted to be. It was something that naturally unfolded because I was already on a path of accountability. COVID amplified all of that for me. Not only did I begin to "sea" more clearly, but for the first time, I began to listen. When still, my electromagnetic shield is down, and I can hear what other people are saying. Their words are no longer sitting on the surface layer of my prickly skin. When my guard is up, the outside world is not able to sink in, and this places me on script where I materialize reelality.

Anytime we are negatively charged, we hear through our *fear ears*, which challenges rather than aligns with reality. When in doubt, all we hear and see is mistrust. Our fear ears, along with our third eye, are activated.

Four Corners of the Universe

There were several consecutive weeks during COVID when I visualized (with my eyes closed) seeing my organs smiling (I'll explain more at the end of this chapter). At the end of each session, I was drawn to sending loving smiles to each of my cells. I covered my eyes with my hands and the vision often resembled an evening sky lit up with thousands of fireflies. Within a few days, my imagination witnessed hundreds, if not more, tiny golden bubbles (or orbs) parting from my ears. I completed this meditation several times the year before but had not experienced anything like this.

The orbs took me back to the time in eighth grade when I stood in front of my school locker. I was always late—not because I didn't have enough time to get there, but because I was afraid of going. School terrified me, as it shines a spotlight onto our inner and outer value by grading us. I felt like a failure most of the time, and the last place I wanted to be was where I felt that was thrown in my face.

Because I arrived late that day, there were no students or teachers in the hallway. I opened my locker, took out the books I needed, and as I shut the door, I clearly saw several transparent, metal-like silver orbs floating in front of my face. My first thought was that it wasn't really happening, that things like this only happened in movies.

I stood watching them for at least 10 minutes, in part to make sure they were there. Each time I reached out to touch one it moved away as if it were playing. I wanted to stay because I felt safe. A teacher shouted my name from the other end of the hallway, startling me. To my surprise, the orbs were still there. As I reluctantly walked away from them, I looked back over my shoulder until they were no longer in my sight.

When I met with the golden orbs during COVID, I experienced the same feeling that I did at my locker—I felt safe. I didn't understand what they were or why they had appeared and wasn't trying to figure that out. It felt natural for me to enjoy the moment. A month or so later, I came to know them as the four corners of the universe, or the closed and opened mind.

At first, I visually noticed the orbs in my imagination—not like in eighth grade when they appeared outside of me. This led to an inner conversation with the four that I later realized was me in Soul center. The more emotional scales we peel off our skin, the more we "sea," and therefore know. When we are in our ghost body, we're in the closed box. All thinking is the box. When we are in a Soul center, those four corners are unfolded, allowing us to receive life.

When the corners are sealed, we cannot see our way out of a stressful situation; all doors read *dead end*. However, when the box is unfolded, all doors are open, and we go from no way out to having multiple ways out. Not knowing what to do turns into a variety of possibilities. That is what trust provides—a knowing that we are always supported no matter what corner of the mind we enter.

For a while (up until my dog Abby passed), I stopped going to bed worried and, instead, looked forward to it. Due to my feeling safe (trust), I was able to get into bed relaxed. This allowed me to think more clearly, which led to me asking the four (my inner self) to give me either a symbol or a word to questions I had prior to going to bed. I awoke in the morning knowing the answer. Similar episodes continue to happen. Trust has a way of showing that.

During the first week of the four entering my life, I sat one morning trying to meditate (or what I thought was meditation, trying not to listen to anything). But my next-door neighbour was hammering and drilling in his backyard and it sounded as though he was in my living room. At first, I felt extremely irritated and began fantasizing about going outside and telling him to shut up. I was about to go and ask him politely to quiet down when I heard, "Let all sounds in."

The words did not feel separate from me as they had when I thought I would die just prior to entering the whiteout. This was my own voice speaking to me, which I mentioned, happens when I am in my instinct. The more in my physical body I am the more I connect to the whole self. Now words no longer seem separate from me, they are me.

I immediately felt my physical body relax, allowing me to breathe more fully, as I was unaware of being physically tense. When we're unaware, it's easy to lose sight of where our physical bodies are and move into our astral head to suffocate and choke on the stressful story. I later found out my neighbour had made all that noise because he was building a waterfall to bring him more peace. He'd learned that his liver was failing and decided it was time to make healthier choices. Had I disrupted his peace for the sake of my own, it could have negatively impacted us both.

Before that, I had never thought to let in all sounds. In my previous meditations, I had been in observation of my thoughts. But it never had occurred to me to listen to the room I was in, whether there was noise or not. I tried to drown out my headspace with my breath or a mantra while oblivious to listening to anything outside of me unless it entered to disrupt activity. Then I'd tell myself to relax and not pay attention, which only added more resistance and prevented me from taking it in.

In the past when I meditated, I believed it was about going inward. The thought of going outward didn't occur to me then. I came to realize it's opening myself to the outside first that allows the *in* to unfold.

It's not about trying to relax but rather being open to the outside. When I am open to the room, I listen through my collective ears. I'm connected to the room, which is no longer separate from me. As difficult as it is to describe this expanded being-ness has an authentic sound similar to ringing in that it feels like a rise in frequency.

In this state my hearing feels heightened and there's vibration everywhere, though it's not merely a sound. It's a genuine feeling as though I were standing in a giant subwoofer and feeling its vibration. As the sound rises, there's a noticeable change in the atmosphere now inside me and coming to life. I feel like I've turned inside out and merged with the room.

The sound resembles the fabric (which I define as the ether) of the room continually spread open. It's a kind of unfolding that feels and sees in my mind like a book being opened in the middle with its sides curled back toward its spine. It's a deep widening of energy I feel everywhere in my body, sometimes more dominant in specific areas.

When the box is unfolded, ether flourishes. Ether is the fabric of the tiny golden bubbles. It's what makes up all life. I would go so far as to say it is the blood of all life and what connects us. When our collective ears are switched on, the sound of ether rushes in. It is the sound of all existence.

Listening for Connection

I believe we can all hear one another through this connected sound. This is how I can sometimes receive messages from other people's consciousness. We are all connected to one another, but doubt prevents us from knowing this. When certain bodies of consciousness communicate with me, they are not telling me the person's future. They come to tell me where they are in that moment. When we are in rhythm with the endless beginning that is all there is.

The people who come to me are typically still alive, though people who have passed on come to me as well. When the deceased arrive (and this is rare), it's usually to ask that I pass a message to someone else. When the living's consciousness arrives, it's to pass a message to themselves. An example of this is the experience I had with John, as the reelality self of the individual coming to me is not listening to their instinctual self.

This triggers the release of their reality self to search for other lights that are not only *on* but that are within range and able to pass this information on to them. This happens when a person experiences a moment of vulnerability (as how John came to me). There need not be a life-threatening situation for this to happen, but there must also be a moment of emotional lowness (vulnerability) that inspires the light part of themselves to intervene.

Pay attention to how you perceive the experiences I share with you. I hope to remind you of how, when we let the ghost in, it can dress things in a way that removes us from the experience. When we read something or listen to someone else's experience, our minds automatically make it a movie for us to watch. This can put us underneath the story, making us feel small and the person telling the story seem big. We make a much bigger production of the person's experience than it may be, and that can make us look for something that's not there when we decide to take on the experience. This forces us to miss out on our own experience of it. Subtlety is key.

Over the course of the next several months after I began listening, I felt more comfortable wherever I went. Outer sounds did not have the same impact on me they once did, and I began seeing them differently. I found that when I'm triggered by an outer sound, like words spoken to me, I know it's not the sound that's bothering me but what I decide to name it at that moment. Words become painful only when we weaponize them. Remembering this turns the words back into sound, and now there's simply a sound that is no longer a threat to me.

Listening is something that has changed my life in profound ways. I practice it in my seated meditations and wherever I else I may go. I no longer feel obliged to sit and close my eyes to listen. Like anything practiced, it gradually becomes a reflex. It now comes on spontaneously at different times during the day and at night. Much of the time I don't see it coming, and it's a pleasant surprise, putting a smile on my face. It appears when my brain is overthinking on autopilot. I immediately feel calm, supported, and safe, like my life in that moment has purpose and meaning. I move from arguing with the moment to feeling completion within myself. I do, however, still enjoy meditating in the mornings when I get up. I find it helps ground me into the seat of my throne.

I no longer meditate the way I used to. There is a vast difference between trying to concentrate on one thing versus listening to everything. One turns on the astral mind, and the other connects you to reality. I now know that when I listen, I am unfolded, and when I don't listen, all I hear is ignorance.

When I let all sounds in (lasi), I do not deny or halt any sound that wants to exist. From the moment an uncomfortable thought enters our minds, often we don't want to be thinking it. We don't allow what we hear to manifest, refusing to let it be as it is. What makes any thought insufferable is not allowing it to be heard. For me to experience peace and quiet in my life, I must let all sounds in. Without it, the script will only get louder. Our fear ears will only grow wider, pulling in more fear to squeeze us with.

There were many years when I heard my dog, Abby, breathe, it would make me hold my breath. She had a challenging time breathing due to her respiratory issues. I listened to her struggle and felt panic. I wanted to fix her but could not, and that led me to feel powerless, which broke my heart and enraged me at the same time. However, when I began listening more often, her breathing softened. This does not mean my wanting to help her breathe more easily was any less, but it enabled me to hear it from a different perspective—one that I had not thought of before.

Knowing is trust, and trust is instinct. Animals are ghost-free. They sit rooted in their instinct, their minds knowing that if their bodies become sick, it is a part of an evolutionary process. They do not emotionally fight the disease, allowing it to manifest. It is neither right nor wrong, but rather complete. When something is complete, it is in total trust.

Humans can be seated in their instinct, but it's more a choice than a natural reaction. They argue with what is, as they are addicted to their outer senses and dependant on the environment to make them feel happy.

Animals show us how it is possible to effortlessly live our lives, which is one of the many reasons why I love having them in my life. I now understand when I do not allow Abby's sounds in, her condition (in my astral head) gets worse, and this prevents me from being with her. Before Abby passed away, I made peace with her respiratory sounds and was able to connect with her. This is the only real way I can be with her. Anything outside that is reelality spinning out of me.

Examine whose life it is you may be trying to control right now. Notice the words as they surface. How do they make you feel? What happens to your breath, your muscles, your digestion? Does it make you want to scream? When you feel a power outage, your solar-plexus chakra is activated, enforcing a loss of control, which (because of the root chakra) makes you feel the need to control. Let's go through an exercise that can, when you're willing, refill this void but let me first explain a point.

The more powerless I feel, the louder the words become. This makes me want to raise my voice along with tensing my body. When I raise my voice, I'm unable to hear the words in their natural state as opposed to sound uninterrupted by fear. Words hurt when they are weaponized. When all we hear are bullets and bombs, we're prevented from hearing the real sound of the words, which have feelings. If we have war words with us and are unable to access the feelings contained in them, it is important that we speak to them peacefully – internally and externally – so that the feelings contained within them feel safe to come out. This allows them to be felt and accepted back in by us.

Trust Your Journey

When doubt is switched on, it puts us into a state of mistrust, which makes us not only distrust our personal journey but the journeys of those around us as well (as it was with Abby, always needing to fix or save her before I started listening).

Therefore, so many of us cannot bear to think of someone we love suffering. We tell ourselves their journey is not meant to be happening even when it clearly is. We throw reactive and repeated emotional fits but not

SITs that exhaust our life for us and, in doing so exhaust the life force of those around us including the one we want to save.

The only reason why we would not trust someone else's journey is that we're unable to trust our own. Our well-padded minds are of the belief that they know what is best for the other person (no trust), as if to say, "my Soul knows more than yours." We then become unable to get out of our own way and choose to barricade ourselves in front of someone else's.

Take a moment to feel how exhausting that is on all levels. Feel how hard it is to prevent the ones we supposedly love to have their own journey. Where there is no trust, there is no love, no matter how much we try to convince ourselves otherwise. The ghost will argue this endlessly to hold us prisoner to the idea that love is pain. Keep shining the spotlight on the ghost's conniving, or it will veer us off course and have us remain victims.

Close your eyes and relax your body for a moment. If your head is full of words that want to get out, let them out. Keep in mind that you're in control of the words. Once the words are out there, they lose power and don't hold as much control. Feel your breath as you inhale and exhale, not to distract you but rather to give your brain what it needs to provide you with clearer perspective. Feel it rise and fall and rise and fall again. Continue for a few minutes. Feel the words land on your skin as sound. Keep your body relaxed. Place one of your hands over your solar plexus, you're *in and out* point of power. This is where you read energies and where you allow other energies to read you. This is the center that can eventually shrink you, especially when you want to remove burdens or save others.

You need not hold your hand over your solar plexus but keep your attention there. Let the sounds you are struggling with enter. Remind yourself of what you innately know, which is that the person's life you want to control has the right to be here exactly as they are. When you convince yourself they do not have that right, you not only take away power from yourself but also from them.

The need to control is a loss of control. *I know I am in control* says that I trust where I am. This allows me to connect or be with those around me, without infringing upon their journey. This is real support; this is what love is.

Notice if you tense your body by resisting the thought. Relax your shoulders. This exercise is more of a listening meditation not a SIT (which can trigger the release of physical movement). When the shoulders are tense, they barricade the heart, which blocks the lungs. When we don't want to feel something, we purposely use our shoulders to block the emotion, adding more heartache. In time, this can lead to heart or lung issues.

When we fight for something, we can't break bottom (or be vulnerable and in Soul center with those we love). When we fight, we sit at the bottom, not breaking it (total loss of control/unconsciousness) and transform into a *wrinkle* (pit of withdrawal) that inevitably pulls everyone else in the same vibrational vicinity down with us. I mentioned earlier, trying to remove burdens from people results in hurting them and us.

Place your hand over your solar plexus and breathe calmly into it anytime you feel threatened by your thinking so that you can let the war out of the words. Words fill up with reality oxygen and turn back into sound. Keep relaxing your body and imagine light under your hand. Remember that *you* are your source of power!

This exercise helped me immensely when I was caught up in one of my mother's memories. Growing up she shared several of her childhood traumas with me, stories that I took on as if they were my own. Placing my hand over my solar plexus, I spoke out loud. This is not my memory, it is my mom's. Therefore, you are not welcome in my body—leave now. Then out of nowhere, I experienced several sad low sounding moans, followed by a floodgate of tears. Underneath the words came the sounds of the feelings that, prior to that moment, were held hostage by the story (war words). Often, we take on the pain of others because we don't understand how not to. This exercise realigns us to our point of power.

Letting our loved ones have their own journey does not mean we stop loving them, but rather that we *are* loving them. As a society, we tend to have a complicated view of what love is. We grow confused, thinking that with love comes pain. Many of us tell ourselves love means we must beg and grovel and prove our love to one another. That if someone is hurting, we too must hurt so that they'll know we love them. To love is to let go and let happen. When we hang on too tightly, we cannot breathe.

The ghost can be sneaky and try to hide things to keep you astral. Notice if you steal someone else's sound when trying to unburden them. Remember (snap yourself out of being hypnotized) that it's their sound. Keep reminding yourself that to be a supporter to your loved ones, you must allow their sounds to be theirs.

See the bent noise in the sound leaving your solar plexus now. As you speak, moan, or tone the words out, see them being released back into the ether to be recycled and unburdened from you. If you feel guilty, know this: guilt enters only when you're not seeing correctly. Guilt, then, is asking you to have another look at your situation—one that encompasses a panoramic view. Guilt lets us know when we are off course, as all negative emotions do. Redirect your attention back to knowing you're allowing your loved ones' sounds to remain their own.

Now feel your point of power filling your solar plexus area. Feel the joy and relaxation. Feel the anxiety alchemize to relaxation. When you do this, your point of power radiates outward from you in support of those around you.

Meditation Part One

Listening to the Inner and the Outer

It's important that we remain consistent with exercises that help us remain grounded in our physical bodies. When we don't, we suffer.

As I write this book, there's extensive construction going on outside our house. I too am doing a lot of building, and it only makes sense that the outside reflects that. Because I have chosen to let all sounds in as well as SIT, the construction noise has not bothered me. Nothing breaks when you listen. When our fear ears are turned off, our collective ears are on. Now it's possible for all sounds to be weightless. When all sounds sink in, we have decided to allow them to do so. This decision deactivates our prickly coat, making way for us to take in every sound around us. Now we are really meditating!

The only reason many people are unable to heal themselves is because they cannot *hear* themselves in an expanded state that merges with life. When focused on the outer as a distraction, they are unable to get past it and, instead, make it louder and harsher.

When I meditate, I listen to all outer sounds, this enables me to accept all inner sounds. Not only that but I allow myself to feel the effects of those sounds (the emotions and emotional impact they may have when they rise to the surface). Meditating this way is a great precursor to SIT 1 and 2.

I do not observe my emotions like I was taught in yoga instructor training because I understand that only digs me a deeper hole to crawl out of later. I don't observe my emotions because that is a way to deflect from feeling, which only attracts what I want to get away from even more. Whether that ends up being more mental suffering later or if I get good enough at ignoring my emotions and are mostly numb to them, the resistance may appear as misalignment in my physical body.

Instead, I go straight into the emotion and remind myself to listen, which automatically enhances my breathing and enables me to feel and thus drop into any tension that comes up. When I meditate, I relax my body and mind so that I am more able to take in my surroundings. Do pay attention to whether your using meditation as a way to avoid feeling or open the door to it. Are you relaxing to escape feeling? For me, I use meditation for a variety of things, but mainly it's to be more in body where my feelings are. Alternatively, stories tend to float above our heads in *outer space* like a cartoon bubble, pulling us out with them. Becoming attached to words can disassociate us from feeling and healing. When I'm trying not to think and attempting to avoid being triggered into my feelings by not *listening*, my relaxed state will be temporary. The SIT methods show us how to gain access to our feelings in a way that can, when we are willing, give us more permanent results.

When I let all sounds in, I don't try to surrender per se. When I try to surrender there's resistance, which means I have my electromagnetic shield up. That makes sound prickly against my skin. Instead, I remain open to all sound and in doing so, sound can penetrate, reintegrate and become a part of me. When I remain open, surrender naturally happens.

The ghost seeks excuses to make you uncomfortable. Rather than getting bent over it, "sea" how it is helping you. Look around the bend and "sea" that behind every uncomfortable noise, there's a waterfall being built. When you convince yourself that the condition (whatever it may be) is bad, you unfailingly need it to stop or be fixed. This turns an alarm on in your head that makes you feel possessed. It's important to remember that when listening to that alarm, your electromagnetic shield is up, and now nothing you want can get in. You may hope and pray for the right doctor, medication, or something else to come your way, but with your electromagnetic shield up, it cannot get to you. You cannot *be* love when you are blocked. When not in your point of power, you inescapably turn into a consumer, and a consumer does not grow anything but simply takes.

You cannot be a battery until both ends are put together and you "sea" out what pains you.

Life constantly unfolds, and with that unfolding chaos can sometimes occur. You cannot have a positive without a negative—at least not as far as reelality is concerned. You do not clean up one mess while thinking all are now cleaned. Life is a constant sweeping. You are either the person who picks up the broom and sweeps or the one that gets swept over.

Be kind to yourself. The more you choose to berate yourself, the more you wire and fire that which you do not want. This, like all things in life, takes practice. The more you do, the better you will feel because you remember where your physical body is. Thus, you will personify your point of power, which enables you to truly be with those around you.

Smiling Organ Meditation

Smile as you place your hands over top each of these organs: brain, heart, lungs, liver, kidneys, throat, and stomach or anywhere else you feel drawn to. Choose any kind words you'd like to say. For example, "We (you are a system of trillions of cells) send you love, joy, abundance, and eternal smiles." Or "I love you and appreciate you." If you feel you've been hard on a specific organ, or organs, you could say, "I love you. I'm sorry for hurting you in the past. Please forgive me," or anything else you choose. Just keep in mind that words don't heal. Vibration does, which is why I have also found it effective to focus on a specific body part and listen. When I feel aligned to do so, I'll make sound, like a hum or a moan or a tone. Let yourself listen to what the body part feels like without trying to change it. Be supportive to how it feels. This will enable a safe place for it to feel accepted by you, which in turn will help you be more accepting and loving of *all* of yourself.

Chapter 10

MEDITATION PART TWO

There are many different types of meditation. Not too long ago one of my meditations took place in Faber, Virginia, at a place called the Monroe institute.

The Monroe Institute (MI) from my perspective is a school for expanding consciousness. It has in-person retreat locations in Virginia as well as online courses. According to their website, MI uses, "specially designed binaural beat audio-guided technology." It is my understanding that this specially designed technology can enhance the meditation experience. Since I wanted everything wonderful to happen instantaneously, this concept appealed to me. I believe there are many people who, like me at an earlier point, want everything fast—even meditations.

In the past, meditation was annoying, but only because I was waiting for something miraculous to happen. I wanted to reap the benefits from meditation sooner than later so that I could get on with being happy and healthy as promised (or so it seemed to the ghost). This mindset bypasses reality and goes directly into reelality. We want our lives to happen in a flash without realizing that *in a flash,* our lives are gone.

Prior to my going to the MI, I'd experienced merges with the other side. In a merge, we don't move out of our bodies, we stay in place, though merges can be confused with out-of-body experiences.

During an out-of-body experience, we move outside of our physical bodies. This reinforces the astral realm, but not reality. Leaving the physical body is a spiritual event, which is, fundamentally, a spiritual quest. There's nothing soulful about it. All it will do is feed the hurried, unsettled mind.

The ghost loves to move fast, and when given something that will get it to its destination quickly, it will leap at the opportunity. The remaining problem is that it will never be satisfied. Once given a fast-track route, it will hack all occasions after that. Where there's an absence of attention paid to the present moment, we find the ghost. When not given what it wants immediately, it throws a fit. The ghost cannot sit still because its outer senses seek stimulation, and its thinking is restless and ungrounded. This mind moves fast, dragging the body behind it like a ragdoll. Being bored is a lack of attention span to the present moment. To the ghost, it feels like time is slowing down. This makes it feel restless, so it comes up with all sorts of excuses as to why it can't stay where it is.

When we take the time to unmake time (self-care our way through doubt), we are not in a hurry to arrive at certain destinations, attain spiritual or educational degrees, or have material things. We may still feel burdened by the same stressful thoughts, but since we consciously try to resolve them, we don't feel nearly as overwhelmed by them. We experience where we are and that unfolds the box.

MI awoke the E.T. kid in me that craved the MI awoke the ET kid in me that craved the fantasy/reality life over the reality one. Each time I visited the institute, I looked forward to meeting and getting to know the participants who gravitated there from all over the world. One might think that such a place would attract all sorts of weirdos, and it did. But it also depended on whom you might think is weird. The people ranged from the military, government, pilots, big-foot trackers, alien abductees, engineers, scientists, doctors, psychics, and authors, among others. There was never a dull moment and always someone to talk to.

I enjoyed getting to know the facilitators. Most were kind, supportive, friendly, and interesting. Many had their own adventure stories to tell. Everything about the facility, the programs, and the participants were fun and adventurous. Being together in one big house made it feel like a family get together at Christmas.

The Meditation Experience

The meditation experience shared here involves me joining together with one of the groups. These people included other attendees, a woman named Mary, and her husband, Frank—who had crossed over. I'd met Mary once prior to the session at the beginning of the week when we introduced ourselves. At the time of my meditation experience with her and her husband's energy, I was unaware she was married and had a deceased husband.

Before we get into the details of what happened, let me first describe what the set of a session looks like. We met in the common room. The instructions for the meditation session were explained by the facilitators. We then went to our rooms to meditate. Our sleeping area was also where we did the meditations. The beds were shaped like pods and closed on all sides except for one to allow for climbing in and out. Once in bed, a black curtain is pulled shut to block out all the light. The pods are not as claustrophobic as they might sound but are rather cozy and comfortable.

Each pod has an on-off switch that lets the facilitator know when we are in our pods and ready. After each meditation (depending on whether we do back-to-back sessions), we met back in the common room to share our experiences.

There are generally four meditations per day, sometimes five, lasting between 45 and 60 minutes. Bob Monroe (the creator of MI) passed away many years before, but his presence remains, possibly in the astral realm. Most meditations use a recorded voice of an instructor to guide the participants. I would point out here that what everyone sees and experiences during the meditations is their own experience. We are guided by the recording to different focus levels (platforms of existence), while being instructed on what to do when we get there. The instructions themselves are minimal. What we see and feel when we arrive at these places, has its own view according to our perception.

Prior to this trip I had completed two back-to-back programs at which many unbelievable physical and mental experiences took place. Each weekly program is designed around something different. One week's program was based on guiding Souls trapped in the astral realm so that they can move into the next stage of their evolutionary process, or what some might call heaven.

At the start of this meditation, I spoke aloud to whomever or whatever was out there, saying I wanted confirmation that what I was about to experience was real—not only for this specific meditation, but for all the others I had experienced in my life. At that time, I was still in a deep state of mistrust.

Almost immediately after addressing the universe, I felt my right hand expanding, which was not something foreign to me. When meditating in the past I've had similar things occur, which I later came to realize were the beginning stages of an out-of-body experience.

Soon after my hand energetically grew, I felt the unmistakable sensation of another person's hand holding mine. I followed Bob's voice and found myself standing in a white, cracked-mud desert with a blue-skied horizon.

Meditation Part Two

I looked around and took it all in for what might have been 30 seconds. Then, out of the blue sky, a white horse appeared.

I approached him and stroked his head and face. In my mind I could feel his hair. I stared into his eyes, and he gazed back at me as though he was looking through me. I climbed onto his back, and he turned and rode us high into the sky—so high that we broke through it. We were flying then galloping across a sandy beach. We traveled between worlds.

A few seconds after landing on the beach, Mary seated herself before me. I could only wonder what she was doing there. This was a Soul retrieval, and since she wasn't deceased, seeing her was confusing. I climbed off the horse and sat next to her as she opened her hand and showed me the solar system. She said what I believed in my heart was true—that the solar system isn't something outside of us, but is instead something we all innately hold inside of ourselves. Therefore, we have control over it.

I sat mesmerized by the image of a galaxy swirling in her hand, but then grew distracted by a man standing in front of us. He extended his hand to me, and the two of us walked across the water together. He was bald, muscular, Black, and had the gentlest of ways about him, as if he were an angel. We walked for only a few seconds until Bob Monroe's voice said it was time to move on to the next focus level. "We are now moving on to focus Level 21," he said, and the beautiful man let go of my hand. I fell downward through the ocean floor and out onto a golden level. Everything, including the sky, was the colour of gold, including the grass, swaying like seaweed. It all appeared as if it were under water.

To my left, Mary sat in a tall, throne-like chair. She wore a long, gold, sheer gown embroidered throughout with lace flower patterns. Her hair was styled eloquently, with sheer pieces of fabric flowing from it. This image of Mary did not match the woman I knew. She had short hair, wore no makeup, and dressed tomboyishly.

I watched her and felt an energetic pull from my right side as she rose and walked in that direction. A man stood across from her. My heart skipped a beat at the sight of his dark, curly hair and piercing green eyes, and I instinctually knew his name was Frank.

I watched their eyes brighten at seeing each other. They wrapped their arms around one another crying in real time and space while I lay in my pod. I felt everything they felt and was swept away in the magic of their moment. I had never experienced that profound depth of emotion. I love my husband dearly, but this was different. Perhaps that is how love feels on the other side (when it's not being contained by a conditional body), or I had felt the extent of their mutual love all at once. The emotion possessed my entire being in the most beautiful way, and I am eternally grateful for it.

Frank held her tightly and said, "Mary I love, love, love you—I always did love you and I always will." His confession only made me cry harder, making my body ache. Tears of joy streamed down our faces. We were in this realm together. I was aware of them and feeling their emotions, but they were not aware of me. *How is this possible? Is this my own love or is this their love?* I felt confused and unable to understand how their feelings were flowing through me.

I wanted to stay in that moment with them forever but was interrupted by the instructions heard in my headset. Bob's voice informed us it was time to move on to the final level, and we immediately moved to Level 27, assembling in front of a door showing that number.

This level can be seen however you want to see it. Some might see it as heaven, and for others, it might be another dimension or something else. The number on the door was the age at which I experienced the whiteout.

The door opened and the three of us walked into a massive golden coliseum where we, (more Frank, I believe) were greeted by hundreds of cheering people in stands. The room was bright and full of warm hearts, and Frank's face showed a joyous expression. He turned to Mary and handed her a letter, which, as she opened it, released dozens of bright-coloured butterflies that flew out and filled the air. The letter read, "I love, love, love you."

Then it was over. Bob's voice began counting down numbers from ten to one, bringing us out of hypnosis. At the sound of one, I lifted my headset, ran to the bathroom, and fell to the floor. My roommate was still in her pod, as there were still two meditations left to go, but I couldn't endure more after everything that had just happened. After 10 minutes, I splashed cold water on my face and headed outside. My heart felt fuller than ever before. I didn't know what to do with this immense outpouring of energy. It felt too big for me.

When I walked outside, I was still crying, and when I looked up, Mary was walking towards me. Dumbfounded, I didn't know what to do at first. A part of me wanted to turn and run, but I couldn't move.

"Hello. Jennifer, is it?"

"Yes," I replied. "And you're Mary."

Without warning, words flew out of my mouth. "Mary, did you have a husband that died?"

"Yes, why?" she asked, looking startled.

"Did he happen to have black curly hair and green eyes?"

"Yes! Yes!"

"Was his name Frank?"

"OMG, yes!"

She immediately wrapped her arms around me, and I returned the hug. We both cried and fell to the ground. It was one thing to know her husband had died but to also know his hair and eye colour and his name, was something else. Also, Frank is not the most common name.

"How do you know that? Tell me!"

"He entered my meditation just now, and so did you."

"I don't understand. I was in your meditation with you and him? But I didn't see either of you in *my* meditation," she said.

"He may not have been in your meditation with you, but he was in mine, visiting you. I was just there witnessing it like a conduit."

I went on to tell her about the letter and the words written in it. I told her that prior to my seeing her on the beach, I had been escorted to her by a white horse. She then explained that she and Frank had owned a white horse. The two of us sat in the dirt, laughing and crying at the same time. She told me that Frank's death was a suicide and that only days before it happened, he had mailed her a letter that she received the day after his death. It contained the words, "I love, love, love you." Mary and I wept for hours afterward.

What disappointed her was that he had come into my meditation and not hers. I explained it had to be that way for us both to honestly believe the occurrence was real. If he had entered her meditation, it would have been easier for her to later wonder if she had made it up. When we love someone and they're gone, the desire to see that person again can be so great it can blind us to knowing what's real and what's not. His coming to me, a stranger who knew nothing about him, would be more plausible.

She understood, though could not help but feel disappointed that she didn't have a similar experience. She was not there to look into his eyes or be held by him and she needed that. We all need love and affection. They are the most desired emotional states for us to embody while we are here.

Being a part of and conduit-to, what I believe is an incredible love story, is something I will always cherish and be grateful for. Not only did I get to feel the love Mary felt for Frank, but I also got to feel the love Frank felt for Mary and at the same time, which broke and then opened my heart. I had the combination of both their love for one another. It filled my heart to the point where it expanded, which is what the breaking and painful part was. It was also an experience that, like meeting Betty, not only enabled me to feel more connected within myself but also to a total stranger.

The love between them coursed throughout my veins as though it were my own. It proved to me that we really are all one mind, one big ocean of love, and when we are open to receiving that connection, we *runneth* (a word used to indicate a person having more of something they believed they could have) through one another and become one.

Expanding my Experiences

I loved visiting MI, and when I say this, I am simply sharing what unfolded for me afterward. This in no way should suggest you be fearful of exploring it for yourself. When I returned home from the first two programs I took back-to-back, I wanted to drink alcohol. I went from having zero desire to a hundred reasons why I should drink. MI did not make me start drinking. I simply point out here how forcing the brain into certain oscillations un-naturally can stir up other things. I believe that these brain-altering sounds did have an influence on my situation but only because I was already in a power outage. If I were not mostly out of my physical body, I wouldn't have gone to MI. The ghost looks for ways to strengthen its hide.

I believe that MI helped bring to the surface what was still unfinished in me, and that this time, it was up to me to resolve, without the whiteout's assistance, what was still there.

When I am not in my physical body, I am in the astral realm, which means I am controlled by cause and effect. What I do in this fast-track lane will have consequences. But when I still myself into my physical body without trying to get somewhere, instead taking in where I am in the moment, I am consequence free.

I have found that the more oblivious to my thinking I am, the more I question and need proof of things—the very reason I needed validation that my meditation experiences were real. The more I let all sounds in and SIT, the more quest-full and questionless I become, although this does not mean I am not still curious.

A question begs to draw information from someone to learn rather than know. Ignorant thinking energizes a top-and-bottom bunk relationship that can remove a person from their instinctual self. Curiosity, however, stems from an instinctual awareness that innately knows that the outer is the self. Curiosity then bridges the gap between the word's teacher and student. This is how people can undergo healings from others. When instinct is turned on, all life is able to move through us, making it a conduit to us and us to it.

Chapter 11

INFLAMED THINKING

When the mind is lit, the body will be lit with it.

On a physical level, the astral brain gives us all manner of gut issues. We are not genuinely in our bodies but rather roaming in *outer space*, leaving them on life support. When we are in our instinct, we're connected to our brain because it is in our gut. The brain in our head follows its lead.

What's your gut health like? I know mine was terrible for years. Halfway into my three-month trip in India, I believe I contracted a parasite. My stomach grew increasingly bloated and continued mostly on like that for 10 years. The parasite was confirming my real emotional state rather than how I was pretending to feel. That's what our physical bodies do to show us what our thinking looks like.

Because I was trying to think my way out of how I felt daily, the negative charge surrounding my mom along with everything else that was painful in my life gestated in my gut. Because I was genuinely wanting to mend the pain, my gut grew increasingly bloated over the years to show me what I was ready to give birth to. The same goes for disease. Disease is the physical manifestation of suppressed emotions. It surfaces to show us what we're ready to emotionally process. Unfortunately for some, they don't see it that way and instead see the disease as something bad that they need to get rid of as soon as possible. This makes us resist the disease more, which can be painful and even quicken the deterioration process.

Had I not had genuine intent to repair myself, the pain would have stayed suppressed in a flat gut like it had for years before and could have quite possibly manifested into something more detrimental to my health. I've found that ignorance (trying not to face something) is not something that leads to bliss. Instead, it is something that leads to unwellness. Looks can be deceiving, which is why it is important we do judge a book by its cover. When we don't, we remain ignorant to the feelings wanting to be born.

Take advantage of the ghost's mindset. It shows you the negative charge surrounding the feeling and gives you the in. Judging a book by its cover is to our advantage when we use it as ammunition to fuel the fire during a SIT. This way we don't remain ignorant to what's inside of us when we do get triggered. If we try to talk ourselves out of how we feel by "looking for the spiritually evolved answer" we miss out on accepting and thus transforming how we really feel.

The Physical Manifestation of Emotions

Back then, the thought that "all physical ailments are emotional" only fleetingly crossed my mind. Information sat more on the surface layer (electromagnetic shield), remaining something learned but not known. It didn't become something known until years later during COVID after I let all sounds in and rewrote my childhood. During that first month of rewriting my childhood and letting all sounds in, SIT 1 entered my life. I believe it was this combination that made my mind and body less bloated. It was also during that time that the information pertaining to all physical ailments being emotional sunk in and went from something learned to something known. Prior to that, the charge I was holding up against my mom prevented the understanding from sinking into a knowing.

I believe our intestine (which is divided into two sections called the small and the large intestine) is where our emotional body (feminine side) resides and that when we don't see our emotions through, it can give us all sorts of gut issues. This includes things like bloating and endometriosis, as well, any other gut related health issues. These physical ailments manifest when we suppress how we feel. I call the gut the God brain because it is my belief that the gut instructs levels of different chemicals in the brain. Chemicals provide emotion. It is where our instinct resides (hence the term gut instinct). Therefore, good gut health makes us feel giddy, energetic, and even euphoric.

The more we accept our emotional body, (something we do in SIT 2) the more we accept our physical body, as the two are interconnected. This brings me back to what I said earlier regarding my struggles with food. Before Abby passed, I was still mindlessly overeating. Then when Abby passed, my body went into a state of shock and began, to my great dismay, reacting to food much differently.

I went from eating whatever I wanted (without any stomach irritation) to suddenly being forced to be very selective with my food choices. Also, my body wouldn't allow me to overeat no matter how hard I tried. And trust me, I tried! Then one day I decided I was going to SIT with it. From that moment on, my eating habits began to change for the better. This does not mean they are perfect—it means it's better than it was. To make a long story short, "SIT-ing" instead of giving into my cravings when I wanted to eat poorly or overeat exposed the emotions hiding behind the usual hangry emotions I'd feel before a meal.

Once I got passed the frustration and anger, grief came in and took me on a whole other rollercoaster ride that I wasn't expecting. I couldn't see the hidden emotions before that because I never gave myself a chance to fully feel the hangry feelings (frustration), let alone any others attached to it. In my early 40's while my mom was reading me a letter of apology (she wrote to me in my 20's but never gave to me) she said the only time she ever recalled holding me as a baby, was when I needed feeding.

From the moment I could feel the food tantrum brewing, I would eat to medicate and numb myself from having to deal with it. Not realizing that in the process I was emotionally vacating my body. In doing so, I was feeding my astral needs, giving them more power to control me the next time around. It was during my SIT with food that I realized my desire to overeat stemmed from my desire to be held and loved by my mom.

Some people don't take care of their bodies with proper nutrition and aren't working out or exercising because they think since Soul is light and it's not coming with them when they die, what's the point in trying? This of course is just another excuse not to feel and take care of ourselves.

Remember what I said earlier, the body is the Soul. If it wasn't, we wouldn't have one. Think of your body like it's your Soul because it is. SIT with what's eating you up inside and your astral mind and body will feel full.

An overgrowth of bad gut bugs can lead to anxiety, depression, paranoia, and all feelings of inner alienation. My lack of self-acceptance and trust within myself led to an overgrowth of what some might see as foreign invaders but are instead parts of our astral self's way of showing us where our emotional head is at.

Let's say that you contract a parasite. Your *outer space* head would want you to believe you have a foreign invader in your body, so that it wouldn't have to take responsibility for attracting it in the first place. Whereas the mind would see the parasite as a physical manifestation of suppressed feelings. What's in us is ours when we argue that we suffer. The more we don't take ownership of our mind and body, the more we are run by them.

Think of it this way. When we are digesting our thinking, our bodies are in digestion mode and we're not being run by old programming. When we don't digest our thinking, our guts become sluggish, stagnant, and backed up. When our guts are moving too freely like with IBS (irritable bowel syndrome), it's the same thing as being constipated. We're off center. Come into alignment with your emotional body (God brain) and whatever's out of alignment, will correct itself. The more I feel, the more I trust my gut, which is why I don't need science or other forms of information to prove my beliefs to me. I also feel less inclined to pick up the phone to ask friends what they think I should do with my life or a situation. When I feel, I trust, and when I don't I mistrust and *need* everyone to tell me what I should believe and feel.

When we suppress our feelings, we unknowingly push them down into our gut like a garbage disposal that eventually gets backed up. Since the gut instructs the brain to produce chemicals to match how it feels, the more we deny the more unwell we feel.

Emotions cause illness when we're either trying not to feel them or we're beating ourselves up for having them. This is still a form of not feeling our feelings in their absoluteness. For some, it's the blame these emotions are receiving that's making the body sick, not the body making itself sick or the emotions themselves causing the body unwellness. At first, emotions can cause sickness, but not when there is acceptance. When we stop making how we feel wrong, illness, even if it's still there, becomes non-existent. While you might still get cancer and not recover from it, but since you unconditionally accept the feelings surrounding the cancer, you pass peacefully. This may be difficult for someone who prides themselves on being positive because to them, an unwell person is someone who has failed at being positive. This is another absurd way of thinking that provides a lack of light and an abundance of suffering.

Sometimes, the more we uncover emotionally the worse we feel. I believe this is what a healing crisis is and is our body's way of purging the old so it can be transformed into new—similar to my panic attacks. So, if you're applying some form of mental and emotional self-care to your routine, you may experience uncomfortable physical symptoms because of it. This conversation may shed some light onto why this is happening and enable you to feel less resistant to the process. Just remember to keep in mind I'm reminding you I am not a medical practitioner. If your feeling unwell, please consult a physician.

I have heard many people say over the years that they want to get back to their old self or feel young again. Needing to physically get back to someone your clearly not in this time zone puts you on the clock. The past is in control of you and your asleep to its programming. Replace those old, tired, and life force depleting words after you've seen them through with "I feel new" or "I feel repaired and renewed." Becoming newer is you in alignment with the eternal beginning. You're moving forward without force or resistance to change. Unconditionally accept the lack of self-acceptance that is leading you to believe that wellness lives "back there," and you bridge and repair the gap between time zones. This is a present state of mind, which, like everything else we think, the body downloads and mimics. When you fake saying something, you inflame the words, which when spoken repeatedly inflames the body.

Unawareness is the threat that imposes inflammation on your body and warrants special attention to how you react when new information is presented. Whether we are stressed or in denial of self-acceptance, our bodies become inflamed. This happens through both our conscious thoughts and semiconscious scripted thoughts (DNA).

One way to imagine inflammation is a hot temperament or an emotional flare up that causes a physical flare up. But we don't need to be angry for our bodies to be inflamed. In fact, anger often means you're moving through something harsh that's on its way to something less harsh so long as it is something you are in the midst of seeing your way through (SIT). Otherwise, anger can bring an increase of inflammation. When we are on autopilot to old conditioning it oversees us. We are not present. Lack of presence activates the sympathetic nervous system. This activates stress hormones that can cause poor mental and then physical circulation—all of which are indicative of and promote inflammation.

People are attracted to cold therapies because it helps them feel less physically hot or inflamed. But it does not get to the core of the issue. The reason why people continue back to cold therapies is rooted in their thinking rather than their bodies as they might believe. Cool you're thinking and your physical body won't need cooling.

When we see our inflamed thinking through, we don't require cold therapy to feel better but until we address the essence of the flare up, the physical inflammation will keep coming back no matter how many cold showers or ice baths we take.

I noticed over time that the more I felt and accepted my pain, the cooler my body became. I went from cranking up the air conditioning before bed each night because I was so hot to not needing it most of the time. The more so-called negative feelings I accepted in myself, the less inflamed and hot I felt. When I understood this, I also understood how the same theme played into my menstrual cycle. When I resisted feeling my cramps by taking an anti-inflammatory, I learned nothing about my pain. I would continue to feel emotionally all over the place a week or two out from my period each month.

Epiphany of Pain

Women have been taught to believe that menstrual pain, hot flashes, and brain fog are natural parts of a woman's evolution and aging. I agree, it's a part of aging. Therefore, it only happens when time is in control of us and we're in reelality. What's important to point out here is whatever the emotional or physical distress is, it's brought on by lack of feeling. Physical distress then, is our body's natural way of trying to get rid of the static from the negatively charged belief.

As a society, we have made women out to be the ones that get to cry, or the ones that are crazy and unstable for crying—especially during menstruation or menopause. For example, "The reason I feel emotional is because I'm getting my period," or "I'm eating this way because it's that time of the month," or "I can't go anywhere or do anything because I'm mentally and physically exhausted from my period," etc.

What some of us may not realize is that the reason we feel emotional during these times and sometimes use it as a way to excuse our actions during it is because we're not allowing ourselves to fully feel both our emotional and physical pain during this time.

Throwing a small fit or crying in small bouts or screaming into a pillow doesn't allow the feeling to be fully realized. Chaotic emotions are a sign the hormones are out of whack and the only reason hormones are not harmoniously flowing is because the mind has yet to be in harmony. For the mind to be in harmony it takes self-acceptance, which requires outright feeling.

An unwillingness to experience feelings puts limitations and conditions on acceptance. As we now know, we cannot be unconditional with anyone when we're not unconditional with *all* of ourselves first. Until we allow ourselves to fully embrace our feelings, we will continue to have little outbursts toward ourselves and others. So, whether we're holding our feelings in (like the stigma around men has been to do) or being chaotic with them, both ways are conditional and strengthen chaos, rendering us reality blind.

Here, women are being given a life altering opportunity to clear ancestral pain (pain that is passed down and recreated). The more we feel our menstrual pain, the less heavy the script feels. Unconditional feeling releases pain that our ancestors endured. Today is the ripe opportunity to feel and transform the pressure they felt that was stemming from their inability to feel their own pain. Not because they weren't strong women, but because like so many of us, they weren't instructed how to experience their feelings unconditionally.

Many of these women were not allowed to have a voice. They were taught to shut up, be quiet, and to do as they were told or there'd be consequences. Women also had to hide how they felt—not just for their own safety but for the safety of their kids. We are in a much different world today, though there are still some places in the world where women are unfortunately still required to live out these chauvinistic and abusive times.

It's important that we get that pent up energy out. Some examples would be to cry, shout, moan, roll around, stomp, or all the above. Otherwise we hold it in, which is never a good thing because it can build and fester, causing further emotional distress later. For myself, there are times when I add subtle movement like rocking myself in the fetal position, and other times (as mentioned in chapter 6 when I SIT), I lie down perfectly still and don't move a muscle or make a sound.

I have had equally profound moments both ways. When I say profound, I'm not implying that light shoots out of my head or something dramatic. After having done this often, there are times where I find myself swept away by the grace of it, wowed at how the pain shifts from one emotion to the next and can bring memories from this life and other lives.

To be honest, I look forward to my periods. They have become a sacred part of my womanhood. I've learned from feeling my pain versus resisting it that I am stronger in a way I never knew before. I feel comforted and closer to my female ancestors, and that helps me to feel less alone and more supported. My monthly cycle, and possibly my menopausal cycle one day, will continue to be felt by me, and therefore remain sacred ceremonies within myself. I use the word sacred because it implies a connection to God (or the gods). Therefore, when I feel ALL of myself, I combine/unify both sides of my battery (divine feminine and divine masculine). These ceremonies may appear on the outside to be occurring alone when in reality, I have thousands of strong women backing me (ancestral lineage). These women are not behind me in past tense. Because I am allowing myself to feel all of myself, they are right here with me.

Rather than feeling the pain our monthly periods bring, many of us use medications to numb it out and suppress it instead. It is my opinion that taking pain medication of any kind during menstrual cycles numbs and disables us from being able to clear our pain today, as well, a long line of ancestorial pain, therefore we remain operated by it. This is another reason it keeps coming back the next month. It is my belief that unresolved pain prevents our body's natural ability to produce light, which is why many women feel so mentally bogged down, physically heavy, and bloated during menstruation.

In the past, menstrual pain, to me, used to feel like pressure. That's all I really knew about it. I wouldn't allow myself to go beyond the pressure because I'd take an anti-inflammatory within minutes of me feeling it. Up until my late 30s I would cycle between taking Ibuprofen or Midol to suppress the pain. Then one day when I could feel my cramps coming on, I decided not to take one. It had been so long that I couldn't remember a time before that when I didn't take one. Within minutes the cramps felt overwhelming. My mind raced. "Should I take a pill or should I not take one?" I kept asking myself but instead of giving in, I continued to feel the pain. The more pain I allowed myself to feel the more I began to see. Let me give you an example of what I mean. One of the first times I allowed myself to feel my menstrual cramps, I was shocked and amazed at what happened. I had an epiphany.

The more I allowed the pain to consume me, the more I could see parts of myself in other lives being poisoned, beaten, raped, and imprisoned. I also experienced the memory of being burned to death for being a woman who used nature as her medicine. I could see blood streaming down every part of my body including between my legs. This made me question whether bleeding during menstrual cycles is physically necessary or is a by-product of the mental bleeding women were subjected to while being suppressed, since I believe that everything begins in the mental body.

Lifetimes of oppression flashed before my eyes in mere seconds as tears rolled down my face. My stomach was in knots and my body trembling and weak as if I were there. And yet, in that moment I was—or rather those lifetimes—were here with me in this time zone. Lifetimes where women were deemed witches and burned at the steak for being mothers of the earth. Medicine woman who could not only hear the animals and the land speak to them but were also instinctually guided by them to help heal themselves and those around them. I cried for what felt like an hour in that morning. I didn't stop until the many faces of me were exhausted. I consoled all the hers that I saw. I held her, loved her, appreciated her, and in doing so I consoled, held, loved, and appreciated me in that moment also.

When we grieve, console, nurture, take care of, and unconditionally accept our oppressed female ancestral pain (or any pain for that matter), we rewrite our timeline and are no longer controlled by a past many of us are unable to consciously recall but still feel. The more we feel, the more our perception of how we feel changes. For example, what we thought was chronic pain, may shift into something noncontinuous. Pain that comes and goes.

We don't get rid of anything, we transform it. Because energy can't be destroyed, only transformed, when we don't allow ourselves to feel our pain by numbing it out, it still goes somewhere in us. If we are suppressing how we feel, we're not accepting that part of ourselves. "I only want to feel the good feelings" vibrationally says I don't accept the bad feelings. Which means I'm being conditional. As long as I am being conditional with myself, I will continue to be conditional with others. This subject pertains to all pain, not just menstrual pain. When we unconditionally feel, we can drop into all sorts of pain from different time zones. Some of us will feel and even see racial pain, religious pain, pain from having land taken away, etc.

In the early stages of me not taking any anti-inflammatories, I felt intense pain. But the more I allowed myself to drop into the pain and truly feel it, the less emotional suffering I felt. Therefore, I don't feel the same way about my pain. This does not mean that I do not still undergo pain—I do, but not nearly as much or in the same way.

In sharing my experience with you, I'm not suggesting that you should give up your pain medication. That is up to you to decide. For me, when I refuse to feel uncomfortable and continue to reinforce the behaviour pattern by taking pain meds, I notice the story about my pain seems scarier. Notice how I used the word *seems*. My pain seems scarier, but since that's the story I'm telling myself, I can't know for sure because I've taken something to numb out the actual knowing. I've already made up my mind the pain is on its way. From this perspective, pain is either remembered or anticipated.

I'm not saying that all pain can be eliminated this way. Like I said, that's up to you to decide. You are the one that decides what's best for you. Ask yourself when was the last time you allowed yourself to feel your menstrual cramps? You may find after reading this you feel inspired not to take a pill the next time your cycle comes around. If that is the case, remember to inhale and exhale into all your feelings. If your mind is willing, it will tell you the story.

Unity of Male and Female

Women have come a long way in the last hundred or so years when it comes to career, equality, and politics. But where we have yet to grow is in unconditionally accepting our feelings. If men felt safe to allow their feelings to move through them, they too could embark upon sacred journeys within themselves that would lead them to experience, embrace, and accept their today pain as well, their ancestral male and female pain. Pain that both men and women feel from their mothers and fathers.

To think that only women are allowed to embark upon sacred journeys throws the mind off center, creating a gap between the mother and father God inside of us.

Men may find that when they dive into their own sacred journeys of physical or emotional pain that they have memories of being persecuted or tortured in some way just like some women will. Men may have their childhood come to life and remember feeling forced to be a man in some way. An example is being forced to play contact sports like football or being forced to hit somebody. Basically, feeling forced to do things that felt out of character for them that then quickly became accepted and encouraged behaviour, throwing them off their emotional body center and Soul center.

Men have been shamed into thinking that emotional expression is not manly. The problem with this is it stunts men's inner growth and emotional movement along with their own self-acceptance. Lack of self-acceptance equals young essence—meaning an adult body but minus the grown-up essence. This is why I believe as a society we have become accustomed to thinking that women mature faster than men.

The more feelings we suppress, the more immature we are. This of course applies to both men and women. I have met many women (including myself) that grew up with an emotionally unavailable mom and their essence was immaturely suppressed. This suppression can make some men and women feel resentful, protective, and defensive (which remember, has you in attack mode) towards women. To them women reflect that which they so desperately want to be but are conditioned not to be.

Just because I'm a female in this life doesn't mean I'm not affected by the hurt from the male side of my DNA, or that it doesn't get switched on when I'm triggered by something in my environment. What is in our script is ours. Just because I haven't spoken about my father in this book doesn't mean I'm not harbouring pain. I've just realized that the pain was hiding underneath my mother pain. I've only recently began seeing my way through the pain of my father and am still in the process of it now. It's not something I'm ready to share just yet, but will quite possibly in the future. What I will say is there's a lot more there than I originally thought. I'm realizing I was much more oblivious to my father pain than I was to my mother pain.

For me, there's greater strength in facing fear and terror than there is in avoiding it. Many women tend to look at their period like it's a burden, when in reality it can be an opportunity to move feelings. Men should be able to have the same opportunity and set aside a few days per month to feel out their own emotional or physical pain—be that masculine or feminine or simply embracing whatever comes up.

When we accept all of ourselves, we no longer undergo someone else's suffering (ancestral script) and carry the weight of their burdens. We understand suffering is the effect of not feeling. If we are unable to honor our bodies just as they are, our bodies will continue to feel rejected and unaccepted by us. How can we unconditionally accept all of ourselves when we are being conditional with some parts? Conditions kick us out of the body. When we unconditionally accept all of ourselves, we're not trying to change anything.

Regardless of your sex, we all occupy an energetic womb. We're all capable of birthing ideas and projects. The act of physically giving birth may live in the female body, but because it is energetically a part of the whole self, it lives inside all of us.

Having shared some of my views with you, it's important that we don't try to force our opinions onto one another. Thinking you know what's best for someone else and trying to force that on them might not go over well. For example, me telling my husband he should set aside a few days per month to get to know his feelings might backfire on me, making him irritated. If he is not wanting to "sea" his irritation, he could hold me responsible for making him feel that way.

For some men that would be like asking them to put their hand on a hot stove and hold it there for a few minutes. No one in their right mind would do it. Remember, someone else's readiness is not dependant on you, and when you try to force something, it can blow up in your face. Because force is different than suggestion, sharing what you're doing or what you read in a book is different than telling, and can have more power to influence.

Emotional Awakening

Soul Center is the centering of God father-mother.

I want to back up for a moment to something I mentioned earlier. For me, more recently, I've been experiencing what feels like an uprising of feminine energy, or what I also call God mother energy, and I believe this is due to me seeing my mother issues/pain through. I have also noticed others around me are feeling the same way, so this may be something taking place on a global scale. I mentioned in chapter one how during the whiteout I heard two voices, a man and a woman, and how when they spoke, they did so at the same time. This was the first time I became aware that God, universe, or whatever you choose to name it, was not just male.

The reason they spoke at the same time is because they're one state of be-ingness. There's no separation between them. The same thing happens to us when we are in emotional harmony. We merge and embody both our feminine and masculine sides. When we are in emotional chaos and not accepting all of ourselves, our energy splits and we feel incomplete. This is the reason why so many are in search of the perfect partner to feel com-plete. We are seeking completion in balance with someone who can fill in the gap, when, really, we need to find completion in ourselves.

When we don't resolve the projected internal affairs between the mother and father within us, we either make our parents wrong or God wrong. Then we project it onto the men and women in our lives. Refusal to reflect upon our lack of self-acceptance makes us want to point the finger *out there*, which only makes the gap wider and thus more painful.

Think of the ghost as the emotional stalker. She's always trying to inspire you to feel something you don't want to feel, while the mind does its best to positive talk you out of it. God Mother, divine feminine, or emotional body are the negative side of the battery. God Father, divine masculine, or mental body is the positive side. They both have negative and positive aspects within them.

For example, when mind tries to positive talk its way out of something, it does so because it genuinely wants to help. Little does it know that it denies accepting a part of itself and ends up creating more lack. The same goes for the ghost when she tries to make you feel negative. She doesn't realize because like mind, she too is cut off from her whole self. Triggering you to feel negative makes you not want to accept that part of yourself and again reinforces a lack of self-acceptance. If mind and ghost were one, they would not be trying their best to tear you apart. It does not matter what you call the emotional or mental body. All that is required to merge with *him* or *her* is a desire to feel and see your pain through.

For me, what is taking place behind the scenes that my human eyes can't see is the war between mother and father within me is being resolved. This means a merging between the two is occurring. The split between them has been going on for so long it has made the gap for many of us more familiar. This can be challenging for those experiencing the same uprising of energy, because not only can it make you feel emotionally chaotic, it can also leave you feeling physically exhausted (healing crisis). On the other hand, others might feel more physically energetic and emotionally centered. One is not better than the other though, as we all process information uniquely.

Our feminine side does not apply only to women just like our masculine half does not only apply to men. The two live inside the same body and as mentioned, split up when there is an imbalance between the two. God masculine may be what some experience next after the feminine, whereas others will experience it the other way around.

The two are inescapably heart bound together so no matter the order, the more the old conditioning rises, the more you will be experiencing some form of the gap closing.

To believe God stays the same and never evolves limits him/her and makes God finite.

I believe that God is like all of us and is always learning and growing. The more that we understand this, the more we embrace God within us and re-alize that *He* is us. Not only that, but we stop blaming the men and women around us for our problems and we understand they're unaccepted parts of ourselves that require internal nurturing.

When we're in alignment with all that is, we don't have to wait for tomorrow to start something mental or emotional over (for example, thinking we have to go to bed and then wake up to reset the day) because we understand every moment is a new beginning. When we're in Soul Center, we are always beginning.

The combination of all four methods shared throughout this book (rewriting your childhood, letting all sounds in, and SIT 1 and 2), have been, for me, necessary to be able to unfold the four corners of my universe. They have tuned the frequency of both my mind and body cells (holographic and physical) to be in a state of receivership more often. I also have them (mainly SIT 2 and lasi now) as tools for the next time I lose sight of where I'm at. This allows me to explore the new findings along the way back to (which remember, is your current time zone) my whole-God self.

My SIT Experience

To close the chapter, I'm going to share one of my SITs with you that occurred just a couple days before my period. If you're a woman reading this, you may have a better understanding of how I was feeling because for me, five days or so before my period is generally when I feel most sensitive and sometimes overreact.

On this particular night, I had some friends come over for potluck dinner. We usually had a girl's night at another friend's house, but she'd recently sold her property. Her house was on a beautiful piece of land, and because she was a home builder and a designer, her place looked like it was straight out of a magazine. I love my place but the more I focused on her home being the better house to entertain in, the more insecure I felt.

The entire time they were over all I could think about was how my house wasn't good enough. After my friends left, I went upstairs to my room and began crying. I knew it wasn't a regular cry—I was entering into a SIT, and so that is what happened. Keep in mind that how in my sharing this story with you, I want to explain how some things can sound trivial when looking in at them from the outside but be the exact opposite when we're experiencing them.

Initially, I thought I was crying because I didn't have a big or nice enough house to be proud of. But the harder I cried the more was revealed. The energy shifted from me feeling insecure about my house to me thinking my friends were rejecting me, which led to the many times I felt rejected and insecure in my childhood.

"I hate myself. I can't stand who I am, I hate being me, and no one likes me. No one's ever going to like me. I'm hopelessly unlikeable, I'm a terrible friend, and I'm rude, ignorant, arrogant, and grossly insecure." I couldn't stop the words from reeling out of me, and I didn't try to control or stop them. Since I understood the process of the SIT, I fully allowed my feelings to move.

Rather than judging myself and putting restrictions on my feelings, I honored them because I understood that everything that was reeling out of me was ready to come out, regardless of how immature it may sound. I was going to be there to catch and support all of it. I wrapped my arms around myself and loved myself for everything I wanted to feel with no conditions. Halfway through the session Chris came home from his night out with friends.

I heard him come in, but I kept crying anyway. Chris knew about the SIT at that point and always gave me space to do what I needed to do. He came up stairs, walked past me in the bedroom, and closed the blinds. Then he sat down next to me on the bed and put his hand on my back. For a moment I felt comforted by him. But when I looked over, I mistook the look on his face as being irritated. I immediately became irritated too. In my mind the only reason he put his hand on my back was because he felt like he had to show me some sort of support. Now I was angry and resentful because in my mind, my focus on being angry at Chris pulled me out of the SIT I was in with my other feelings.

"You don't have to stay. It's obvious you don't want to be here, so you might as well just go." The victim in me whined.

"You don't know anything," he said, and got up and walked away. And Chris was right. I didn't know what was in his head at that moment. All I knew was what was being triggered in my own head.

Due to what I believed Chris's reaction should have been in that moment (which was to coddle me in some way) even though I basically just told him to leave the room, I became angrier. As I did, I had an epiphany. Just prior to Chris getting home, I felt a bit stuck in my SIT. I was in my feelings but still needed a bit more inspiration. Funny how when we genuinely want to feel better and we apply the Soul work to get there, creation brings us what we need at the exact right time.

Chris wasn't rejecting me—he was supporting me. But because I was already feeling like a victim when he walked into the room, I chose to see it negatively. This wasn't a bad thing because it ended up helping me go deeper into my feelings because I had already had several SITs under my belt. I was more aware of the benefit of what taking responsibility for my feelings could do. When we use the trigger as ammunition to access the feeling, we walk away winning. When we don't, we feel and act like victims. The only one coming to save you is you. Looking to others to do that for you will only hold you prisoner to the past.

To feel better today requires acceptance of how we are feeling right now. If we look for something or someone outside to make us feel better and not do it ourselves, it can push our emotions back down, suppressing how we feel while resolving nothing. This also means we're unable to move forward and be still amidst the eternal beginning where absolute acceptance is met.

This example highlights how to use what we think is a distraction to our advantage. If I convinced myself that Chris ruined my SIT, I would have reinforced that I was being rejected, which would have given the story more power and me less power. Since I seized the opportunity as a way to take me further into it, I deactivated the charge and set myself free.

Ask yourself when was the last time someone interrupted you while you were in the middle of something you thought was important? For example, maybe you were meditating or studying for an exam or were hyper focused on a certain project for work. How did it make you feel to be interrupted and what did you do with those feelings? Did you SIT with them or project them onto the person or animal?

The more stuck we remain on the story, the more charged the story becomes. The problem with this is it distracts us from feeling. When we chase the story, we energetically leave our body. We make the problem denser and, in the process, feel weighed down. The story keeps us stuck in our floating head while watching reruns play out from our astral eye, fighting with someone that's often not even in the room with us. When we get triggered and we use the story to help us gain as much access to the feeling as possible while remaining focused on the feeling, the story let's go of us. Once the feeling has been allowed to fully move and is therefore unconditionally accepted, the charge becomes inactive and no longer bothers us. As a reminder, this, in essence, is what forgiveness is.

Chapter 12

TAKING OWNERSHIP OF PAIN (AND ALL FEELINGS)

I believe that all pain is a desire to not feel. For us to feel, we must first understand how we have been taught not to feel. Think back as far as you can. Can you remember your parents giving you a cookie for having a temper tantrum, or do you remember them giving you a cookie to prevent one? Did your parents support you when it came to you telling them and others how you really felt about them, or do you remember them telling you it was bad manners to express how you really felt?

"Stop your crying. Wipe that look off your face and put on a happy face. Don't act like a baby. Grow up, be nice, stop whining, get a hold of yourself, and act like a good little boy or girl."

Being taught how to act from a young age teaches us how to act but not how to feel—let alone honour and accept how we feel. For example, "put on a happy face," or "be nice," says act the way someone else wants you to act, therefore don't be yourself. Throughout our lives we get good at these acts, carrying them with us into our adult lives and then projecting them in all our relationships. Then, when those closest to us can't read our minds, we throw a fit and blame them for it. At the same time, we're fast asleep to the childhood acts reeling out of us.

A friend of mine calls at least once a week to complain about her boyfriend's lack of psychic ability to read her mind.

"Can you believe it!?" she starts off saying. "He didn't even think to see me on Saturday."

My response to her was, "Did you tell him you wanted to see him Saturday?"

"No, but I shouldn't have to. It's his day off. He should just know I want to see him."

The Wounded Inner Child

When we don't get what we want, our "wounded inner child" acts up and reels out of us. Often this conditioning is active and can make us act like little kids in adult bodies. Let me give you an example from something that happened at the yoga studio recently. A regular participant (I'll call her Suzie) came in and did what she usually does—tell me if the heat is too high or low for her liking. I followed her into the studio to see for myself and when I did, I told her that even though it seemed to be normal temperature to me, I turned it down a bit anyways. Two minutes later a couple other participants informed me that Suzie was adjusting the heat panel.

I politely went up to her and asked, "Suzie, did you adjust the heat panel? That's for instructors only."

"I didn't touch the heat panel," she snapped.

"Suzie, I just had two upset participants come and tell me you did, and so I'm asking you to please not touch the panel again. If you find the room hot, put your mat next to the door. As you know, I often open it during the class to let cool air in," I replied.

Suzie rolled her eyes and waved her hand, shooing me away.

During class when I went to open the door, she said loudly, "Shut the door! It's way too cold in here now!"

Later after class when she came out into the lobby area, I asked her how she was.

"Fine! Whatever!" She said sharply while turning her head up and waving her hand at me again.

"Suzie, I want you to know that I too am okay," I said. She looked at me puzzled (astral eye). "I'm okay with how you treated me before and during class."

"Oh," she said, becoming aware of her actions. For a moment, I could see her settle back into her nearly 60-year-old adult body. None the less, she still waved her hand at me on her way out the door and said one final, "Whatever I don't care!"

Because Suzie had not allowed herself to accept her childhood denial, when she got triggered, the child came into action, and she projected her childish behaviour onto me. Just because we've aged doesn't mean we've grown up. The story I just shared with you is a very mild case of a wounded child being triggered. But if we take a moment to reflect on our own, more severe, wounded child cases, I'm sure we could dig up at least a few examples of more severe cases in ourselves. I know I certainly can.

Couples do the same thing to one another and act like children when they don't get what they want. I had a client the other day tell me that since his wife wasn't giving him what he needed (communication and affection) he was going to punish her by staying in a hotel room overnight drinking alcohol and not answering her calls.

"It's the only way she's going to learn," he said.

"And how has that worked out for you after 25 years of marriage? Is she more communicative and affectionate towards you when you get home?" I asked.

His response? "No."

"Was she ever communicative and affectionate towards you in the beginning of your relationship?" I asked.

"Yes," he replied.

"Okay, so what changed?"

His answer? "Infidelity."

I asked him what her relationship with her father was like. Without going into too much detail, right away he said he couldn't understand why she loved her dad so much considering all the terrible things he did to her growing up.

My response was this: "So, she picked a man that was on a similar emotional wavelength as her father, who would one day show her the same kind of love, an untrustworthy love, a love that would let her down, and a conditional love that would hurt. And since that became her familiar, the data played out of her, and she attracted you into her life." But only because you too have a fear of love program from your past operating you today. And is the reason the two of you came together in the first place—to see your hurt through. That or keep blaming one another and, in the process, remain prisoners to your programming and see nothing through.

He went on to tell me that throughout their marriage, the two of them had been playing games like this back and forth as a means to try and get the other person to bend and give in to their needs.

"Why should I always have to make the first move when it comes to affection? Why can't she be the one to do it every now and again?"

The transformational moment for my client came when he understood that the more he allowed his wounded child to reel out of him, the more he strengthened the same old deeply carved, neural paths ways in his brain that had been operating him for years. This also meant that for a large majority of his day, he was semiconscious to this old conditioning, telling himself he's living in the now while totally oblivious to it.

I went on to explain to him that "one way to change the program you're watching is to do something you've never done before. For example, the next time you're wanting affection from her, instead of starting a fight, wrap your arms around her, kiss her neck, and tell her you love her. If she doesn't respond the way you want her to, still give her space to be in her reaction. In other words, don't interrupt her with an argument that would then cut her off from being able to do that."

She may say, "What the heck are you doing," or "What's wrong with you?"

Remember, you're doing something that's not only unfamiliar to you but also to her and that's connected not only to her father and childhood, but to your childhood also. When you give her space to be who she is in any given moment, you're loving her without condition. In loving her you're also loving you. You're also telling your brain to create new understandings, new ways of being that align to the part of yourself that's holding every ounce of your being together without asking you to thank it.

The more you align to this self the more you actively become it. We don't only create negative programs, we also can create positive ones too.

I went on to say, "It's important to recognize you're not doing this to try and get something from your wife. You're doing this because you want to take care of you, and in that vulnerable space (unfamiliar to you terrain), you expand."

Being in a state of contraction or trying to control your wife's actions and reactions doesn't allow space in you. Contraction collapses inwards leaving very little energy flow. Until you give her space to be who she is, even while in the middle of her reaction towards you, you won't be able to inspire life force to flow abundantly through you. Furthermore, trying to control her will get her guard up in defense mode which, remember, is attack mode and will make you want to attack her more, creating a vicious cycle.

See your wife as your placebo. To help yourself, she is there unbeknownst to her (more on a Soul level) and is inspiring you to feel vulnerable. Then "sea" your way through *it*, through the fiery charge to the water (conscious) side of your mind.

Unresolved stories suck up most of our oxygen, leaving us just enough to survive on but never enough to thrive on. This makes us conditional, and in turn, activates our partners conditional programming.

I went on to explain to him that when you highlight her good qualities, you activate those more and the combative ones less. You are in control of your wellbeing. But the second you believe you must control her, you lose power, which only makes you want to control her more.

Taking Ownership of Pain (And All Feelings)

When we are loving (accepting all of ourselves), we're not in need of being loved. Therefore, our minds and bodies expand and thrive. See your way through that which pains you in this time zone (because remember, you don't have to go back to the past to fix anything) and you will alter the programming of your childhood. Which essentially rewrites your history. Along with this, you'll also collapse the need to have those around you fill your voids for you.

Pause for a moment to observe how your own immaturity has reeled out of you. Be that with your spouse, children, family members, friends, co-workers, or total strangers. When we act like a child today it's because the unresolved comes forward. Remember, when we get triggered into the child and then SIT, we get to support the feelings our child felt back then but in the present. In doing so, we collapse time and the negative charge surrounding the temper tantrum. The past is no longer in control of us, we are in control of it.

When we choose not to take ownership of our feelings, we make others take responsibility for them and we are conditional. Ownership of all ourselves is what leads us to be unconditional and limitless. Think of it this way. For most of us, our hurt today stems from our childhood. The more we shine light onto our hurt today and take action to repair it, the more we heal as adults. Seeing it through allows us to grow up. The hurt child is no longer running around in an adult body answering the emotional wavelengths it's being called to line up with and confirm the hurt in other hurt adult-children. Breakups are endings that occur from a place of brokenness. Conscious uncoupling (from my perspective) stems from a place of wholeness. The couple may no longer physically be together, but since there is no *gap* holding them apart, they are Soulfully one. This is why they can communicate peacefully with one another. They have chosen not to swim in their own ponds. They understand the relationship helped bring to the surface that which required repairing. So, to unconsciously uncouple does not mean we have to remain friends with our ex's. But because we have "sat" with it, we have consciously unburdened ourselves from ourselves through one another and, in the process, become free.

Before we can unconditionally accept our feelings, we must first recognize that our feelings are indeed ours. For example, when I experience anxiety, it's my anxiety because it's reeling from within me. I am the one creating it. Any conversation that argues with reality makes us unable to be unconditional. The feelings remain hidden and we stay unaware. If I say, "you made me feel this way," or "it's not my fault its hereditary (blaming the DNA)," or any other conversation that would deny ownership, that's unawareness. To the torn mind, the present moment is uncomfortable and unknown, which is why very few people choose to vibrate and move emotions there.

Write down a list of the mental and or physical ailments you have. Start each one off with *my* anxiety, *my* digestion issues, or *my* cancer, etc. If we blame the outside world for what's taking place inside us, we lose and the negatively charged belief wins. Remember, what is ours is ours. What we pull in we have aligned to. If you're struggling with taking ownership of your kingdom right now, hold on, we're not done yet. Where there is a will (emotional body) there is a way.

Taking Ownership

Pain is an important subject to shine a spotlight on because it makes it more visible and therefore, less painful. When we try to avoid it, we fear being near it, which can deter us from wanting to SIT with it.

Pain is the argument overriding the feeling and is an active, negatively charged belief. There are a lot of ways we can avoid pain, favour some pain, and create pain. Allow me to explain.

186

Taking Ownership of Pain (And All Feelings)

Ever notice how sometimes we allow ourselves to tolerate some feelings but not others? Or how we think that toleration is acceptance? For example, parents that tell themselves they are supposed to love their children and that no matter what they are not allowed to resent them, or God forbid, feel hatred toward them in a moment of rage. Many parents would rather except the guilt pain than embrace the hate pain because guilt can feel less unloving. If we want to love our children, or anyone for that matter, we must unconditionally accept all our feelings, not just some of them. But just because you chose guilt over hate doesn't mean you've unconditionally accepted guilt. If guilt is making you feel bad, it's because you haven't truly felt your way through it and are instead fixated on trying to not feel it. Who wants to feel guilty? Most of us would rather try to think of something else to make it go away, though often it never does. It only adds to the garbage pile where all the other unseen emotions are.

When we choose not to accept our feelings, we project them onto those we tell ourselves can handle it better, like a spouse or a parent, which then only reinforces the guilt and hate more.

Our feelings are here to teach and help us grow. They are why we came into human form. All feelings are important, and like our children, require tender loving care from us regardless of how we perceive them. Over time when we SIT, we realize this and accepting our so-called bad feelings is no longer a chore but, instead, something we want to address because we know it will make us feel better.

So, instead of telling yourself you'd rather deal with one feeling over the other because we now know that strengthens the negative, feel all of them to the best of your ability. When you do, it helps everyone, not just you. If you want to feel better, which ultimately allows you to be a better parent, it's important to SIT (if possible) alone with your feelings. If you're worried the sounds coming out might frighten those around you, this would be a good time for a quiet and physically still SIT. Remember, "sitting" doesn't have to be a loud and obnoxious event. I previously mentioned I've found just as much if not more success remaining silent and physically still. If you do find keeping quiet stirs up more resistance in you, write down your feelings along with the story line that triggered them in the first place. Then later when you have time to revisit it on your own, you can.

It's also important that we feel and thus repair ourselves for us first. When we do it for someone else, we lose power. Our energy goes out in need of outer acceptance rather than the self-acceptance that comes from within first.

Another way we deflect feeling and suppress pain is by comparing it. The ghost loves to compare its pain to other people's pain. For example, "I lost my job and my spouse left me, but it could be worse. I could have cancer like Mandy or have no legs like John." Ask yourself when was the last time you compared your pain to someone else's or looked for an excuse not to accept your pain?

Remember, pain is pain. It's all relative. But when we use other people's pain as an excuse not to accept our own pain, our feelings get swept under the rug. The more they do, the less we feel them. The less we feel them, the more reality blind we are, rendering us more codependent. "Now I need you to tell me how I feel."

The more we pull away from our feelings, the more *outer space* fills in the gap. This leaves no room for light and that is the part that hurts. Over time we go emotionally numb to the pain and find ourselves in a state of total ignorance, or artificial intelligence. We are now oblivious to the repetition of the movie reeling out of us, which, basically means we become the program (i.e., us turning into an artificial intelligence).

Taking Ownership of Pain (And All Feelings)

The longer we remain under hypnosis to our old conditioning, the more in charge *it* (the negative charge) is. This turns us into artificial intelligence terminals. We become program carriers rather than human beings. Remember, the more we don't feel the less human we are. The longer we allow our negative programming to run us, the more the programming decides who we are.

We cannot evolve when we're looking for excuses not to feel. That's not how life in these physical bodies works. Something I have often heard people say over time is "that's the way it was supposed to go. Therefore, that's the reality of it. If it were not, it wouldn't have happened."

These are excuses and ways not to take ownership or responsibility for our actions. If I can put blame on an excuse like "that's reality, therefore that's the way it was supposed to go," then I don't have to take ownership of my thinking. This puts me into an ignorant coma, fast asleep to reality and wide awake to reelality. I'm living a dream life based off excuses and reasons why I shouldn't have to accept all of myself. It becomes another way to deflect and not feel, and then later, project onto another excuse or someone else. Excuses bolster more excuse making, which strengthen the astral atmosphere which even through our being oblivious to it, ends up hurting us.

We always have choices in life. There is always a brighter path, but when we continue to look for excuses, ignorance keeps us on the darker path. To see the light, we must own all of ourselves first. Then we can begin the journey of accepting all of ourselves.

For us to evolve we must take loving ownership of all our feelings and honour them by allowing them (which is still us), to tell their story through us. We are their host, and they are the glue that decides to hold us together or pull us apart. I'll say it again: all pain is relative. Just because the story of your pain differs from someone else's does not make their pain greater than yours or vice versa. And when you think it does, you'll know who's in control of your vehicle. The second your floating head tries to talk you out of it by making someone else's pain worse than yours, you'll be better equipped to spot it and circle back to take care of your feelings.

So long as we deny our worst fears, they will continue to dictate our lives. Lack of self-acceptance equals conditional equals pain.

It's my belief that all violence is a result of denied feelings. If we all grew up in homes where we were taught that it was healthy to express when we feel sadness, bitterness, resentment, anger, rage, etc., those emotions wouldn't be suppressed and for some, later explode into a living nightmare.

Because we have been conditioned to run from our pain, the last thing we think to do is accept it. The problem with that is, the less we feel, the more dangerous we think feeling is. This is why some people believe it's better to keep things bottled inside. If they express out loud how they really feel, someone, possibly themselves, might get hurt in the process. Know that if you're struggling with any mental issues, you should seek help from a healthcare professional. When we are taught from a young age not to feel and then later in life we try to feel, it can be too much for some to bear.

Unfortunately for some, misery can be quite cruel. What I mean by that is that the more we suppress, the more comatose we can be to feeling empathy. We lose touch with empathy for ourselves and for those around us. Some hurt and kill others, while others hurt and kill themselves in the form of both suicide and terminal illness.

Overcoming Triggers

Terminal illness is terminally suppressed pain. We kill ourselves via lack of self-acceptance. Yet for many of us, we would never think to see our illness as something we are doing to ourselves. We cannot evolve through denial, because as mentioned, it has very little life force and barely moves. Lack of movement creates stagnation which breeds inflammation which in my mind, cultivates disease. When we deny ownership of what is ours, it eventually sinks us into the bottomless pit of pain called hell that lives in all of us each time we try to run. We make ourselves sick by not accepting what's ours. If this triggers you, now would be a good time to let those feelings move in you.

Go back to either SIT method and self-care your way through the steps. Remember, this book is here to help you *lovingly* look at yourself.

When we deny what's being triggered in us by telling ourselves "The other person made me feel this way" instead of "the person helped me to conjure and reveal something unwell in me," we bypass reality and suffer in reelality. I may mention this part again because many of us want to justify being victims because its what's most familiar and therefore feels safest to us. But it's not what sets us free. Authentic accountability for ALL of ourselves with action is what does.

The more we realize the trigger is our call being answered, the more we are able to take ownership of our feelings and recognize the opportunity to heal the pain being conjured. This also makes us less willing to hold grudges against people, which also means we feel less victimized and controlled. It's also important to understand how to use the person triggering you to your advantage. Remember, the SIT method does not require us to forgive those in question. Instead, it shows us how when we take advantage of what they are triggering in us, and use it as ammunition to *See It Through*, we no longer feel the same way about that person.

When we feel tortured by our pain and do nothing to resolve it, it can make us want to torture others emotionally and even physically. Until we *See It Through*, we will continue to place blame on others and make them carry the weight of our pain. Since we don't have control over who or what will answer our emotional outgoing call, it's important that we address that which pains us.

If you have pain right now, be it physical or emotional, ask it to tell you it's story without expecting an answer. For instance, if I tell my pain it's safe to move but have done nothing to prove it, pain will stay hidden and continue to control me. Talking to your pain can be a healthy start so long as you embrace the feedback.

If I say, "Pain, I want to hear your side of the story. What do you sound like, what do you look like," and feel nothing, then I feel what nothing feels like. I don't give up and say, "I'm feeling nothing so it must mean there's nothing to feel." Instead, I'm in denial of feeling, which suppresses the pain further, making me more oblivious to it.

My point is don't try to convince yourself of something that's not there or think that just because you asked your feelings to come out nicely that they will. Most feelings have been suppressed for so long that we've become accustomed to not even noticing they're there until we get triggered into them. If you feel frustrated by not receiving the answer you were looking for from your feelings, that's okay. Emotions are like that. They can shift from one to the next (for example, nothing to numbness to rage) at any moment. When they do, ask yourself if you're willing to seize the opportunity presenting itself or if you will let the frustration stunt your ability to *See It Through* in that moment.

There are many layers to our feelings, which is why if you feel nothing and choose to believe nothing is there, you'll reinforce the feeling of nothing. Just keep in mind that nothing is still a feeling. Once you allow yourself to feel nothing, you might discover underneath of it there might be numbness, which might be connected to grief, sadness, anger, rage, and even terror. The more we feel, the more the mind and body regenerates and fuels life.

Taking Ownership of Pain (And All Feelings)

When I began having panic attacks after my dog Abby passed away, I tried everything and anything I could to make the pain go away: breathing exercises, physical workouts, fasting, praying, energy workers, shamans, my own self-repairing techniques, you name it. I listened to guided meditations when I'd wake up in a bout of terror in the middle of the night, hoping they'd relax my mind enough to put me to sleep, but they never did. Even if I ended up drifting off, it never lasted longer than an hour or two, then the panic would immediately flood back in. It didn't occur to me to feel the panic until nearly nine months in. SIT 2 was born out of excruciating emotional turmoil that became physical turmoil.

There were times when I thought I was accepting how I felt because I told myself I was surrendering to the panic by breathing and relaxing every part of my body. But because I wasn't allowing myself to embrace the fear and terror of the panic, surrendering was just another way to avoid feeling.

Soon after the panic attacks started, I began noticing my blood sugar felt off. I would wake up an hour or two after I went to bed and I'd feel shaky and weak on the inside, but when I'd hold my hand up, it wouldn't be shaking. Oddly enough, my blood work results said I didn't have low blood sugar. The only thing that made me stop trembling inside during those first nine months was sugar or carbs. When I think back to it now, it wasn't odd at all. Eating was my way of filling emotional voids and was the reason why after I ate, the internal (emotional body) stopped shaking.

The emotional turmoil also affected my body in other ways. As I mentioned before with eating habits, my body would no longer tolerate certain foods or overeating. Unbeknownst to me at the time, my body was being recalibrated, repaired, and renewed—like a snake shedding its skin, old to new (healing crisis).

While the panic attacks were happening, my heart would be in my throat beating rapidly, day and night like I'd been running a marathon. On top of that, my stomach either felt like it was in constant knots or a burning pit of flames. Other times, it felt like I was constantly falling, like how on a roller coaster your stomach drops.

Every night I'd lie in bed and put my hand on my stomach. There would be a couple spots where I could feel noticeable hard bulges. As time passed, I began thinking the areas felt numb, confused, lost, and even depressed. At that time, I didn't attach feelings to them. Not until one night during the early stages of SIT 2 as I lay in bed with my usual heart beating out of my throat, a burning pit of horror in my gut, my skin aching, and my mind racing, I realized the hard lumps in my stomach not only had feelings but were feelings.

"Aho, I want you to know that I know you're alive and that you have feelings. I understand you're me and I am you. I want you to know that I'm here for you. I'm going to keep my hand here and hold you. I'm not going anywhere. I'm going to feel you now." What I meant by that was, I am ready and available to connect with you now. The word "aho" is a Siouan language spoken by the Lakota people of the Sioux tribes. It means many things but two of the things it meant to me in that moment were *I acknowledge* and *I understand*. The moment I realized the physical discomfort had feelings, I innately understood and acknowledged it on a whole other level. The sensations were no longer foreign to me.

I allowed myself to feel without conditions or judgment. I didn't say to myself, "Okay that's enough feeling for now, time to move on or this feeling is intolerable, I won't feel it." This allowed me to feel internal movement. When I spoke to the physical sensations in my gut like they were my feelings, they began to change shape. It still felt like a thick snake, but it wasn't scary anymore.

I realized the discomfort I was feeling inside and outside of my body and on my skin all had feelings. They weren't just physical sensations—they were physical manifestations of denied feelings.

A couple minutes later I realized something incredible. I felt safe. I soaked up this feeling like a sponge.

This continued for several minutes until before I knew it, I fell asleep. This was the first time I became cognizant of how when physical and mental feelings are not just observed but felt, they spring to life and literally move. I now understand that when I don't feel everything taking place within me, nothing moves, and everything remains stuck. This is the reason why I feel stuck in a negative head space.

When we resist doubt, we can't move forward. For *it* to move, requires self-acceptance, which is not something that in the beginning we can talk our way through unless we are truly ready to feel.

The more we feel, the more human we become.

Chapter 13

EXPOSING THE SELF

It can be easy to get tangled up in the spiritual mindset that says, "See your-self in the other person. They are your mirror." This can be a distraction. For example, if someone screams and appears angry and then I tell myself I must be angry because they are my mirror, I'm getting stuck in the story of their emotion, not mine. If the person screaming in my face makes me feel angry, then anger is what I SIT with. But if I feel scared, sad, insecure, abandoned, or something else, then they're not my mirror—they are the feeling instigator, and that is a gift. If I tell myself that other people are my mirror, I wouldn't know how I really felt. I wouldn't know my purpose in that moment, which is to see that which pains me through. Go into the feeling that your emotional wavelength collision is providing. Don't try to feel the other persons feeling—feel your own feeling.

After you've allowed yourself to accept how you feel, the negative charge deactivates. You might still think the person is an asshole, but they're no longer the asshole that's bothering you. The reason you disliked them in the first place is because you didn't like how they helped you feel.

Since the person no longer triggers you in the same way, you let go of the old concept you had about them (forgiveness). It's important that we remember that the thank you part comes after the storm once you've used the ammunition to access your feeling. To transform the storm, we must first accept it just as it is. Every emotion is complete until the argumentative mind comes in and decides it's not and tries to convince you otherwise. When we deny our feelings their right to be complete, it makes us feel incomplete.

When we stuff our feelings away and hide from them, we stay stuck in old routines, unhealthy relationships, unhealthy eating patterns, destructive ways of being, etc. In turn, we attract like-minded people (floating heads in the *thrown*) into our lives, not heart minded people grounded in their thrones. When they disappoint us, we blame them because we're stuck in the old, and no light (awareness, understanding, and new information) can get in.

Shed light upon the darkness through unconditional acceptance of your own troubled feelings and not only will you set yourself free from bondage and be unconditional with yourself, but you'll be that way with those around you too.

I know that for me to stop acting so defensively and destructively meant that I had to look at everything I didn't want to look at and get right inside. I had to go to hell to face my demons. When I wasn't seeing my hurt through, it kept me in hell.

We make ourselves hard and dense by pressuring ourselves not to feel. For most of my life, I thought that was my best defense, but all it did was keep my heart shut down, locked up, and in pain. Not being vulnerable hurt me more than it made me strong. I sabotaged many relationships and career opportunities throughout the years because I was terrified of opening my heart to myself and those around me. When I don't SIT with my feelings, I can always count on them to haunt me and run me straight into the ground, time and time again. It never fails.

Reel Self-Care or Real Self-Care

When we're residing in reality, everyday feels like a new beginning. Life isn't pulling us backwards like it does when we're trying to move forward in reelality. In reelality our incessant thinking boxes us in. We have little to no wiggle room and movement to move forward in. This is the reason why, when we are there, we feel stuck.

We cannot overcome fear by pretending not to have it because it will always reincarnate itself. Not accepting one fear filled thought leads to another and another. Since energy cannot be destroyed, only transformed, it will continue to seek forms of transportation to express itself. Energy, or essence, will continue to live regardless of a body's expiration date. The same goes for heaven and hell. Both realms are mental, thus they are energy. So, we don't have to die to go to either of them. We think them, so they are here.

Many of us fear death because we haven't reflected upon our fear and terror of dying. Choosing not to see death through is the very thing that gives death power over us. From my perspective, each time we believe thoughts that place burdensome weight on us, it's coming from within us. We are the ones punishing ourselves and turn reelality (hell) on and our Soul center (reality/heaven) off. There is no bad thing out there that can hurt you— only a state of mind can do that.

For me to *know* I had to face my own fear and terror of dying. Before that, I would try and convince myself that the concept of death didn't terrify me by comparing my experience in the whiteout to it. But the truth of the matter was that I didn't fully die that day. If I did, you wouldn't be reading this book right now. This is an example of how when a program is in charge, it hides and manipulates us into thinking we know something when we don't. This takes power from us, which in turn makes us doubt and fear more. Pause to ask yourself, "What scares me?" and "What am I trying to avoid?" What are you possibly inadvertently covering up because it terrifies you? Remember, what we run from runs us.

The more we practice the SIT method, the less scared we are about life. Time can't control us when we accept all of ourselves. Our willingness to want to change energetically transforms the term self-work into self-care, only having to say the word self-care is no longer necessary. As mentioned, when we resolve our fear around any word, it can't control us.

I've heard people say they're doing self-work, but then when I ask them what that entails, they look at me stunned like a dear in headlights. Self-work, to some, means going to yoga or practicing meditation. But when we're using these things to get away from our feelings, we're doing reel self-work not real self-work. For example, "I need to go to a yoga class to get out of my head" or "I need to meditate to try and stop the head chatter."

Reel self-work focuses mostly on positive feelings. There's a stigma around meditation and yoga that says the more we practice these modalities, the less judgmental we become. But from what I have witnessed throughout my 13-year career as a yoga facilitator, it couldn't be more opposite.

If anything, being spiritual has the power to make people more judgmental. For example, at work I often hear staff and some of the participants say things like, "I only hang around with positive people. I will not tolerate negative people. I only date people that are vegan like me. I only go to these specific yoga instructors because they are better than the others. I never watch TV because it's not spiritual. I only listen to podcasts. I only spend this amount of time on my phone. People that are attached to their phones are unevolved," etc. Sound familiar?

Ever wonder why no matter how much self-work you do, nothing on the outside really changes? That's because in order to change the outside, we must first unconditionally accept the inside. But since so many of us are running away from our negative feelings by trying to distract ourselves with as many positive things as we can, nothing changes. In fact, we often become more ignorant. The more we ignore, the more we bolster ignorance. When I used to use visualization techniques, I would visualize something that made me feel good to try and manipulate a brighter future for myself. This was just another way to escape how I really felt. The only reason we try to visualize a better future now is because we haven't accepted our unresolved feelings from the past. Accept how you really feel (because remember, that's what deactivates the negative charge that's manipulating you to believe you need a better future), and a better future won't be something you're chasing or trying to manipulate into happening.

This conversation leads me to touch briefly on another subject—the Law of Attraction. The Law of Attraction is a philosophy that suggests positive thinking creates positive results, while negative thinking brings negative results. This encourages us to visualize images that will make us feel better now so that we can attract a better-quality life and ultimately be somewhere other than where we are at, regardless of the past. Since what we're running from has more conditioning and layers, it overrides who we are wanting to be today.

Even when some of us do start to gain positive momentum toward a brighter future, it ends up being a challenge to sustain. What's been operating us for most of our lives is what the environment hears most. Trust turns on our receptive mode and doubt turns it off. You can't fake trust—it has to be genuine. For us to trust, we must see our way through doubt and go straight into it instead of trying to get ahead of it and manipulate it. Instead of imagining living in a big house with a beach front view, try sitting in the images and feelings lack provides. If your ill, don't try to envision yourself well when you're not. Feel ill and all the feelings that try to talk you out of feeling ill. Don't just dip a toe in—get your whole body wet. Let the feelings immerse you until they let go of you and no longer zap and control you. All negative feelings feel intolerable until we feel them through.

Meditation often does the same thing, because with it, we are trying to avoid feeling negative. The person meditating in this fashion observes their thoughts. They are watching their thoughts float by, detached from feeling them. This can be an excuse to deflect, not reflect. It's also how meditation can turn into a pain medication (over time, observing rather than feeling makes us numb to our feelings and in turn, sensitive to our thinking). Now I can't tell you how you really feel without you getting your electromagnetic shield up over it.

A Shift in Perspective

It takes a still mind to admit its judgmental ways, especially when we believe we've done so much self-work to improve ourselves. Ask yourself, what self-work do you do and how does it help you reflect and connect rather than judge and deflect, like in the examples I just gave?

As you now know, the triggered event is what inspires the feeling into action. For us to resolve our inner pain does not mean we have to resolve the issue we had with the person. We don't have to make up with or forgive the person or see them in a better light to set ourselves free from the negative charge surrounding the feeling. This is something that can happen as a by-product of our seizing the trigger as an opportunity or inspiration.

It's important that we remember to use the story as ammunition to access the feeling. Otherwise, we might try to positive talk our way out of owning and accepting the feeling. We might say "the person driving me crazy is here to help me get somewhere in myself, therefore I no longer have to see them as my enemy." We try to see the person in a positive light before we have accepted the real feeling rising in that moment—not the pretend one (reel) that our thinking and lack of feeling (not knowing) is leading us astray with. This mindset rejects the opportunity to reflect. Mind has come up with a spiritual excuse not to feel, and yet the only reason we're being triggered in the first place is because we are ready to feel. Thanking the person in your mind or in person can come later after you've taken advantage of the gift they've given you.

Use the story as your starting point and once you have allowed the feeling to fully move in you, the story drops. This is why we sometimes want to thank the other person, though that doesn't always mean we should. Just because you understand how a trigger works doesn't mean they do.

Remember, we answer each other's calls vibrationally. Most of us are un-aware that's what's happening. Stick to doing your own Soul work and you won't need the approval you think you might get in thanking them or try-ing to get them to see it your way. You might find that only pisses them off more and then you could end up right back where you started with them.

Positive talk is everywhere in the world. People positive talk their way out of their uncomfortable situations, pretending life is fun and easy while silently struggling on the inside. That was me for many years. I'd wake up and go to work with the same fake smile draped over the bottomless pit I felt in my stomach. Yoga participants would enter the studio and ask me how I was doing. I'd smile and lie.

I no longer go out of my way to pretend I'm having a good day when I'm not. I don't go into detail about my life either unless it's with someone close to me. Instead, I'll give them a truthful answer minus the story.

"I've had better days, but I'm aware that's the way life goes and because of that I'm working through it. Thanks for asking."

A strangers' response might be, "Is it something you want to talk about?"

"No thank you, but thanks anyways."

Short, simple, and truthful. In doing this I have found truth keeps my emotions afloat where I can better "sea" them and later process them. Responding truthfully may also without trying, inspire the other person to want to be more honest with their own responses.

Exposing negative programming can be life changing when we welcome it into our lives. Running only makes us exhausted.

Positive talk coincides with being non-reactive to our feelings. "If I don't react to my feelings, they'll just go away." This statement couldn't be more absurd. When we don't react to our feelings, they get bottled up. Feelings won't disappear when we ignore them. Wherever they go we go with them because they are us. When we tell ourselves not to react it puts a condition on the feeling. This means our physical bodies won't be in rest, digest, and repair mode.

"Don't react, it's not spiritual," is something denial says to hold us back from purpose. SIT part two encourages us to do the exact opposite: react while in a safe environment without hurting yourself or others as much as you possibly can. Otherwise, you'll remain asleep to the act, and it will be acting you out.

Throughout the years, I've witnessed myself and other people gorging themselves on positive feelings, telling themselves that anything other than positive is not spiritually evolved. I call this mind "spirit captivated." Spirit captivated people are literally captivated by all things nice. In turn, they condemn all things negative, including those they consider to be negative people. The spirit captivated person does not allow themselves to feel negative and instead gets good at only looking at the positive. This unbeknownst to them throws them off center and therefore out of reality.

Spirit captivated always looks for the morally correct response or answer to everything. They are the ones pausing to formulate an answer they think will make them sound more evolved so that they can be outer accepted by their peers. As you now know, outer acceptance comes out of a fragmented mind that is reality blind.

If this triggers you, you'll know where your head is at. Now would be a good time to allow those feelings to move.

Those that only want positivity and don't want negative or even neutrality are controlled by time (unresolved past) and are therefore, confined to the box. They don't want a negative thought because they don't want to feel the charge which, remember, is the emotional body and feminine essence. The more this point is highlighted, the less willing you will be to try and escape feeling, embracing, and accepting that part of yourself the next time a negatively charged belief surfaces.

You cannot be present when you're trying to be positive because you're arguing with what is. Many people preach love and only love, believing that if they stay focused solely on love and sending it out to heal the earth and to those that aren't loving, that this will fix everything. Unfortunately, it won't. When we genuinely accept all of ourselves, we don't *need* everyone to follow in our footsteps. Also, when we are not accepting all of ourselves, we most certainly won't accept other people—let alone be able to change them for the better.

Negative parts are only negative because you've made them negative. Until you accept all of yourself, you'll just be pretending to be someone you're not. Because of that, you'll find yourself needing to save or fix the earth and everyone in it. The more *out there* I go, the less I'll have to look inside.

I also want to point out why there's nothing wrong with being in the ghost body so long as you see your way through it. Then you will understand how it has always been there to help you and was never a bad place to begin with—that it was all always good. There has never been a shadow or bad side. Making the negative bad is what created the void within us in the first place. It's what has pulled the mother and father within us apart and led us to be codependent in our relationships. Which remember is the evolution of why we are here. We inspire/trigger one another into wholeness.

"I have to be nice, good, and holy instead of expressing how I really feel because how I really feel is bad." So, when we don't accept our emotions, our masculine side dominates. Our thinking is now off center, creating more inner separation. What pains us is often a denied part of ourselves that we pushed away that's now wanting to be reintegrated. SIT 2 enables us to feel our emotions through to accept and reintegrate the unaccepted. When we see our pain through, our perception of it changes. Therefore, it's allowed back in, just minus the negative charge. Now we feel emotionally whole, codependence fades, and independence shines. This brings us into union (another word for union is God) within ourselves, which in turn and without need to control others, allows us to be with them (real co-creation). This is why it's important we remember doubt separates the mother and father on purpose to create purpose of expansion, because how could you know something greater unless you experienced that separation first?

Be Honest with Your Feelings

Ask yourself when was the last time you judged someone for not being positive, or were you the one being judged? Do you think you've moved past all your earthly, material desires and are therefore ready to somehow transcend off Earth? The conflicted mind loves to see itself as pure light and as a holy superior. It loves to preach that love is the only way while it remains in total denial of its blame, shame, guilt, and rage. Earth is the projection of Soul-body-mind (meaning earth is the physical manifestation of mind), the belief that you have evolved past it is not enlightenment.

This is an astral thought that has concluded only a part of itself is acceptable, (in this case, spirit), which in turn says, "I don't accept all of myself, only a part." Ask yourself, "Who taught me to believe the intangible was more evolved than the physical?"

Also, enlightenment is not something beyond us that we must reach (like we're climbing a ladder to get to it). It's something that lives amidst the moment we realize total self-acceptance.

Something else that coincides with positive talk is manners. Both pretend to be someone they're not. Whether it's with coworkers, strangers, or family, how often do you look someone straight in the eye and tell them how you really feel about them? It's bad manners, according to a man-made rule, to tell someone how we feel. But manners don't inspire light, and instead block it.

Most of us keep our opinions to ourselves because we've been conditioned to believe it's unhealthy to tell others how we feel. We get good at lying because most of us are taught that lying to someone about how you feel is better than telling the truth.

We might try to convince ourselves it's because we don't want to hurt the other person's feelings. But the truth of the matter is we're more terrified of how we will feel in telling them. Heaven forbid we say something truthful. We might have to feel our feelings, which could be hellish.

Instead, we grin and bear it, listening to conversations that bore or irritate us, patiently waiting for the conversation to end. Until the veil surrounding the word patience has been seen through, it will continue to hold, emit and energetically translate to impatience.

We have made indirectness a part of our culture, and in doing so, have helped no one. Triggers allow us when we are willing to do the work, to remove callowness, and in its place, have new understandings. In other words when we don't do the self-work and we stay at war with the other person, we widen the gap between us and learn nothing new. Whereas when we seize the trigger as an opportunity to reflect, we learn something new, hence how in *its* place fills in new understandings and new information. When an opportunity to express how we feel arrives and we deny it by telling ourselves its bad manners, we feed astral purpose not Soul purpose.

One little lie leads to another little lie that stockpiles into a landslide of lies. Your friend might ask, "Do I look fat in this?" Your response, even though you think she does look overweight, will probably be "Not at all. You look stunning." The next lie comes when you're at work pretending to be happy when you're not. The next lie is to your spouse or your kids. One well-mannered lie leads to another and so it goes until no one really knows who they are anymore. All they know is the reel.

When we make the act of not sharing our feelings a regular practice, like all denials, they end up acting us out. You and I came together to undergo a release of old conditioning via the trigger. When we ignore the opportunity to do that by swallowing our feelings that reason can't be served and transformed into an understanding. Therefore, we're not learning anything authentic. For me, having the intent to heal means that not only must I allow myself to be triggered, but I've also got to accept the emotion from it. Feeling is healing.

When we consciously allow the denial to move through us, the act stops, and we are amidst self-acceptance (Soul center). The only place I believe any of us can truly heal from.

When we're in Soul center, we're connected to all parts of ourselves, we feel grounded, supported, safe, and fulfilled. It is the masterless and, therefore, matter-less part of ourselves that enables form into existence in the first place. Soul center, union or God (whichever you prefer to call it so long as the words aren't in control of you), is mind centered in its body. It's in rhythm with all life and is something that cannot be measured.

If we want to evolve or be more in Soul center, we must get over the belief that we will be persecuted for speaking our truth. When we don't, we feel imprisoned in our voice boxes.

The more I unconditionally accept within myself, and this includes my truth, the less fearful I become. Less fear equals less inflammation. Less inflammation equals more love.

When you look at the chakra scale you can see how not speaking our truths negatively impacts the thyroid. All chakras are linked together and eventually spiral out into other endocrine glands and areas of the body. So many of us feel angry because we're tired of all the lies we keep telling ourselves and others. We're also tired of being lied to.

If you feel angry often, it can be an indication that you're resisting being ready to purge those lies and speak your truth. The more we resist accepting how we feel, the more frustration builds. When we SIT, we give anger a voice by allowing it to unconditionally speak through us. Speaking our truths can also inspire others, like your children and their children, to speak their truths too, and because of it, stand rooted and grounded in the center of their being. If you're going to pass down or spread anything, let it be the truth!

Be Authentic with Your Feelings

When we deny our true feelings, we are unable to feel grounded in our relationships and our finances. That is because we project the same fear over love and money. We fear having both just as equally as we fear not having them. Some of us also use love and money as excuses to stay stuck. For example, "I have to stay in the marriage for the kids' sake, I can't leave this job because I'm too old and my chances of someone hiring me are slim to none," or "I'll never find the same kind of pay." On and on the excuses will continue, so long as we do nothing to change them. Do you feel stuck in your job or relationship? Are you selling your Soul to the devil (negatively charged belief) by believing you're stuck when, in reality, you're not?

Remember, understanding comes from the release of old conditioning, not the reinforcement of it. Your gift to me was what you triggered in me. If the way I want to respond sounds too harsh, then I will wait until I get home where I feel more comfortable expressing those feelings on my own. There's nothing wrong with waiting until you get home to see the pain through. A tip (that I also shared previously) would be to grab your phone and jot down in your notes section what event triggered you so that when you do get home, you have a clear memory of the feeling. Then when you get home, use the story and the feelings that came from it.

I'm not suggesting we be rude in our approach when sharing how we feel, but I'm also not suggesting that we don't. Swallowing our feelings says we don't accept them, and if we are unable to accept them, we are being conditional and are therefore living in reelality. To explain what I mean I'm going to share an example from my past.

When I first began practicing yoga, I used to attend this guy's class where he would repeat throughout the hour how everyone there was not there for themselves. Instead, they were there for everyone else in the room. He'd say things like, "Only selfish people come to class to self-practice whereas the people that were there to serve others weren't selfish and instead, self-less." He would make his presence and his words law by walking over to stand next to whomever strayed away from the exact sequence and then say out loud, "Okay everybody we're just going to wait for so and so to finish up their self-practice so that we can all proceed."

His words were intimidating enough to keep most people in line—not just for fear of being called out in front of the class, but in fear they might be seen as selfish for not caring about our job to be there for everyone else. This might also mean we are less spiritually evolved.

It was during one of his classes that I remember being scolded for doing a backbend instead of a shoulder stand like he'd asked. Within seconds he rushed next to me and in front of the class, said, "If you want to self-practice, roll up your mat and go home," to which I did. I stood up, stared right at him, and said the word "gladly!" Then walked out of the room.

I reacted this way not because I was expressing how I really felt, but because I was too scared to tell him how I really felt. How I really felt had more fire in it. Had I reacted the way I wanted to, I would have called him a control freak and told him to fuck off.

My burning desire to react this way will sound immature and unevolved to someone with a different feeling response or to someone hovering above their throne looking down at me. But it's easier to come up with a response to something that you're standing on the sidelines watching. Also, we're all coming from a different past that contains different emotional layers, and what's important to point out is that both people are emotionally lining up with one another because there are similar wavelengths attracting them.

In other words, we might look at the person pulling the trigger and think that what they said didn't deserve such a harsh response. Yet, since the two of them came together to emotionally duel it out, implies both parties are acting from immature parts of themselves (because the birds of a feather vibrationally flock together). What I think is an aggressive or belittling comment might be the opposite to someone standing on the sidelines watching. What's important to point out is that the two parties came together to instigate feelings in one another. Therefore, no matter how it sounds to someone else, it won't be the same because the two didn't align to share the same experience. However, the bystander may be lining up to undergo their own emotional response. If they are *asleep* while watching the situation unfold, the person may find themselves triggered into being acted out by their martyr or mediator role. Rather than remaining on the sideline, to access and see their own feeling over the situation through. Intervening on something that has no direct relation to them but that they can't help but want to be a part of because they are attracted to certain energies pertaining to the event that will strengthen their old conditioning. Pause to ask, "When was the last time you felt you had to intervene on someone else's emotional collision and what happened when you did? What role was wearing you or were you *seeing it through*?

To think that everyone should react the way you want them to react would be like saying, "My Soul knows more than your Soul. You should live your life the way I live mine." This comment is finite until it is *seen through* and may require the master believing it to face the resistance they feel in not getting what they want out of it.

Ghost hides how it really feels because it needs the applause to feel relevant. Remember, ghost hovers, judges, and condemns those who it thinks are beneath it.

There are two ways to react—authentically and inauthentically. Inauthentically reels out old conditioning, it is void of light, and is therefore an immature act—either brought on by the wounded child or by the moral and spiritual thinker. Keep in mind, embodiment of light stems from the absolute acceptance of a feeling. When we disregard how we really feel by trying to sugar coat it or look for the spiritual response, we are not unconditionally accepting the feeling.

Today, I can see how both responses (the one I verbalized and the one in my head), were immature acts because they reeled from an insecure place inside me that lacked self-acceptance. Therefore, neither of them had been conscious thoughts. The thoughts I was having back then, were thoughts reeling from my wounded child but because I was unaware, I couldn't see it. I was hypnotized by what was most familiar in me. Therefore, my reactions seemed normal to me. Since back then I was unaware there was even such a thing as old conditioning, let alone it being something that can operate us. It didn't occur to me to have a different response. Instead, I was being run from a familiar unlit narrow hallway that I'd been standing in for as long as I could remember. A hallway where because it was my familiar, I felt safe and protected there. Reacting immaturely was all I knew. When I believed I was being attacked and needed to defend myself, I didn't have to think to go to this place, it was a reflex.

My not expressing how I thought I really felt in that moment ended up making me angrier. But only because I was still unaware of being run. I spent months replaying the scene. Frustrated over the regret of what it would have felt like if I had told him how I thought I felt but didn't feel because *it* (the negatively charged belief) was sitting on the surface layer of my skin unable to sink in. But that's what happens when we're semiconscious to the programs running us, we're oblivious to them. New information and understandings can't penetrate *knowing's* when all we sense is the program. From where we are standing everything makes sense.

At the time I couldn't see how sneaky my programming was being when it manipulated me into thinking that holding back what I really wanted to say lacked self-assuredness. Not being able to speak my full truth in that moment made me fester over it for months afterwards. Our old conditioning feeds off stress and anxiety and over a short time, drains our energy. But as I mentioned earlier, for me to understand any of this required time and allot more experiences for me to know myself better.

When I look back now, I see my reaction differently, but only because I've paved the way for new understandings within myself.

From where I'm standing right now, I would have stood up, looked him straight in the eye and said, "Your comment makes me feel small, insignificant, and unintelligent, exactly how my mother made me feel growing up. Because of the overwhelming pain I'm feeling over it, I want to blame you and say you made me feel this way rather than thank you for inspiring me to feel this way. Since I refuse to feel the feelings you're triggering in me, I'm going to go unconscious while my wounded child acts me out, and in doing so, say some harsh words that in my mind, won't allow you to think you're bigger than me."

Again, this perspective is something I realized years later, a decade after resolving many other layers of denial. Therefore, my sharing this later perspective is not me seeking a morally correct response but instead is an example of where (reality) and who (mind) I am today. Thanks to speaking and *sitting* with my truth more today, I can look back and see what was really going on at the heart of the matter, underneath the reactive surface. This is something that can happen sooner and more often the more we self-care.

This doesn't mean that that's where we are supposed to go immediately. Overlooking how we really feel or pausing for the more evolved response only adds fuel to the fire later. Not only that, but when we don't accept how we really feel in that moment, it makes the underneath more reactive next time unless we keep refusing it until it goes numb and we are no longer able to feel it.

I'm not saying we should or shouldn't react this way. It's important to express how we feel, just remember denial hides. It will manipulate us into thinking the good or mature response is the right one when it might be the one reinforcing the underlying feelings to stay hidden. Still yourself to find the real response. Keep in mind your response to certain situations will change in accordance to your self-care routine and the accumulation of your life's experiences.

When I look back today, I can see how I wasn't ready to see him as someone helping me. I wasn't there yet. For that to happen meant I required more negatively concentrated experiences to learn and grow from.

The difference between where I am now when I tell someone how I authentically feel versus the past is now I'm more conscious in my reactions. Since I understand why I'm being triggered (to undergo an emotional wave-length collision), I am confident, clear, direct, and authentic in my response. Whereas back then, I would say things in an arrogant, spiteful way that lacked authenticity because it came from a place of rebelliousness and was therefore less conscious. This always made my reaction sound harsher than it would have been had I been more vigilant. This does not mean that today I look for the morally correct response, because I know that feeds the program. I understand from experience, when I am diligent to doing Soul work (this includes any self-work that pushes me to see myself) and hold myself accountable with action as much as I can, my reactions are much different. Back then, I was oblivious to being stuffed to the brin with old conditioning. I was less aware of there being a panoramic view. The room no longer appears as narrow as it did before. I've noticed after many SITs, my reaction to being triggered has slowed, this has given me time to pause and reflect. Since my thinking is less inflamed, my reactions have less fire in them.

Today, I'm aware of the real meaning behind the trigger. It's ammunition to heal, therefore I understand that when I tell someone how I really feel, I'm helping myself heal something old in me that's then replaced with new understanding. In turn, if the person on the receiving end of my reaction is willing to be honest with their response, it ends up helping us both. And if they are not, it becomes their own issue to work out on their own time.

I also now understand this can't happen when I try to make it based on my time. I don't try and force them to see it from the same vantage point that I do because I understand their readiness is not up to me—it's up to them. Now when I say how I feel, I don't obsess over it for days, weeks, months, or even years. I also understand that without letting all sounds in and the SIT methods, my reactions to life wouldn't be what they are today. I'd still be reacting from a place of being controlled.

Today I understand that real love lives in truth. Pretending to be someone I'm not prevents me from loving all of myself. I have had many scenarios like this one play out in my life before, each involving different places with different faces, and they all had one thing in common—lack of self-acceptance.

How to Use Yoga and Meditation as a Tool

I am now going to close this chapter with an example of how yoga and meditation, when used as a tool to feel, can help us feel more and be more in our physical bodies and make all time happen simultaneously.

For a few years, anytime I would go into little bridge pose (a modified backbend where the legs are bent, sit bones lifted from the mat with hips pressing up), I would feel my heartbeat into a firm area wrapped around my belly button. I instinctually knew there was suppressed pain there, but at the time, didn't know what to do about it. Then, during one of my husband's classes after I came out of little bridge pose, I turned around to face the wall for savasana or corpse (a resting pose which happens at the end of the class) and pressed my feet into the wall. This wasn't something I usually did.

While I was lying there, I became aware that I could feel equal pressure from my big toe through to the pinky toe pressing against the wall on my left foot but not on my right. In my right foot, I only felt the wall from big toe to third toe. Not only that, but I quickly became aware that I felt nothing along the outer edge of the same leg. There was no numbness. Instead, I felt nothing, and that's when I heard myself say, "Okay then, feel what nothing feels like."

Within seconds of my feeling nothing, I was catapulted to a memory of me falling off my bike when I was seven years old and resulted in me breaking my arm. As the images reeled from start to finish, there was a brief, but profound, pause in the middle. My screams were so loud that they caught the attention of my older sister playing at the end of the street, who then informed my stepdad to come get me. When he arrived, he said, "Stop acting like a baby. Pick up your bike and push it home."

Like the words Shirley said to me when explaining the acupuncture needles, "Don't be a baby." This is another example of how when a program is wired into the brain it will continue to seek outer confirmation for its host to feel victimized (via the data being emitted from the electromagnetic field) until the program is "seen through."

I was seven years old and slightly scared of him. I didn't think he'd hurt me, but all adults intimidated me then. His comment forced me to pick up my bike with my other arm and swallow the pain. What I was unable to express got suppressed and was now visiting me in savasana.

Tears streamed down the sides of my face and as they did, I could feel the knot in my throat subside and my entire body relax. As I lay there in yoga class, my feet were still connected to the wall, except now I could feel both of my feet. Not only that but the bulge around my belly button flattened. My point in sharing this story is to show how movement (in this case, yoga) with awareness (a desire to listen and feel everything) can set both our minds and bodies free from things we were once unaware of that are operating us. Before that, I was oblivious to feeling nothing in my right leg because energy flow was being blocked in certain meridians. When we are unconscious of what is running us today, we are unconscious to where its coming from and where it's stored. Had I not already been letting all sounds in as well as feeling them, I may not have been inclined to move into a non-traditional yoga pose that would enable me to feel nothing.

I understand that when I am oblivious to my old conditioning, it dictates how I am feeling mentally and physically today. Therefore, the more I expose within, the healthier I feel. So long as I was unaware to feeling nothing in my right leg, I was also unaware to the *now* memory in charge of my physical body today. Thus, I couldn't be fully present.

So, moving our physical bodies such as we do in yoga (because yoga helps us slow down our thinking by focusing on our breath which then helps us be more aware of our bodies) combined with a willingness to lasi (listen to and feel everything) moves and frees stagnant energy. This can then help unlock different time zones containing memories that when consciously reseen today, turns on repair mode—paving the way for us to spend more time in the present moment.

To further clarify, I didn't need to psychoanalyze the memory to be set free of it. All that was required was me being conscious of the memory and feeling it unconditionally today because as we now know, it's where our point of power (Soul center alignment/repair mode) is.

Chapter 14

MOTHER

So many of us love a good biography, as if writing or speaking about your own life—who you are or think you were trained or educated to be, is going to define who you are today. We are born here with the script printed upon us, and although we cannot escape our DNA, we can rewrite it. When we take hold (remember) our point of power, we alter our entire timeline.

People rightfully love to relate to one another because it helps us know ourselves. If only most people did so for that reason. Instead, they do so based on an opinion about an individual, a judgment call that will determine whether the person fits into their criteria. I want to know your backstory so that I can remain unaware of what is being triggered in me by you. I want to make a judgement call that will deter me from that which I cannot stand in myself, what I don't want to get to know in you because it's sadly there in me.

A timeline of one's life, whether long or short, offers perspective. It gives the boxed mind (intellect) a graph to measure a person's today value with that of their past, but it in no way defines who we are. Who we are is eternally unfolding and is being discovered now in this moment—not the moment before or the one after. Sharing our painful pasts with one another, especially when we are on a self-healing journey, helps expose and resolve what is painful in us. If we see something in another that frightens us, something that tries to convince us to run away, that is our meal ticket in. Running away is what throws us further out and makes us want to throw that same ignorance onto the next person in line. It heals nothing and strengthens everything that's trapped in us.

The path of least resistance is the easier route and is often most familiar. We ignite the emotional imprints that do not serve us but that we keep going back to, because when something feels old, it feels comforting. That is why family (like them or not) is able to pull out of us that which we cannot stand in ourselves. No one can make us feel as out of control as family, and yet, it can also be what is most grounding (both have familiar imprinting).

My Mother's Poem

My mother wrote a poem that she said was for me. It described how beauty was, in fact, a curse. She read it to me when I was in junior high, and directly after, she said she had always been jealous of me.

"It must be nice to look like you. I wonder what it would feel like to walk around looking like you, even just for a day."

These words left me feeling bad and guilty for the way I looked, which, in turn, only made me feel more insecure. It did not boost my confidence in any way. Instead, it cut me down to what felt like a small nub of nothing.

Having my confidence shot down daily put roadblocks around my wanting to go to school and learn. I asked my mother for help with my homework, and when I didn't understand her explanation, she called me a "stupid fucking retard," left the room and didn't come back. Kids are like sponges—they take in so much during their formative years, especially from their parents. Each time my mother chose to call me those things, they chewed through my skin and into the core of my being, burrowing a deep infestation of suppressed bitterness and boiling rage that exploded in my later life. During that time, I had no choice but to tolerate the burning pains of insecurity and low self-worth that only compounded my never feeling accepted by her.

I spent most of my time in school in the principal's office for continually telling my teachers to "go fuck themselves," as well as getting into verbal fights with other students and teachers. Monkey see, monkey do. My mother came to my elementary school on several occasions to yell and swear at my teachers for the way they treated me, holding back nothing, and unleashing everything in front of the class. A small part of me felt vindicated, but it would be washed away in minutes by the rising flood of embarrassment and humiliation.

I never wanted to be a bad student. My problem was that I didn't know how to be a good one. Every day I felt terrified to go to school because I really believed I was stupid. I was frightened of being asked a question in front of the class because I already had made up my mind that I did not know the answer, even if I did. That is not to say that later in life, post whiteout, that I didn't seek education. I did, just not the traditional route.

I mentioned that I traveled long distances to meet with individuals I felt drawn to—not to learn their methods, but to gather inner realizations from them. I needed their placebo effect to help me peel back the harder layers within me so that I might expose, then bear witness to, the lighter inner layers and embody (know) myself (a continual process). Through those inner knowing's, I would come to understand the connection between myself and the outer world (that we are one consciousness).

There were times when I was young when I fantasized about being a doctor or a high-powered businesswoman, but it was always washed away by the tidal wave of doubt. Until my 30s, if anyone were to ask my thoughts on politics or world-related issues, I'd feel an emotional meltdown inside. The same thing happened if I was asked what I might want to do with my life or where I envisioned myself in 10 years. Those questions caused an emotional collapse if only because I already felt broken inside.

I had no idea who I was, who I wanted to be. All I knew was that I was petrified by life and most things in it. It was not until I returned home from a trip to London, England, when I was almost 37, that I began finding my voice. But that's another story for another time.

I always kept my guard up and lived in a constant state of paranoia. I tortured myself mentally from the time I woke up until I went to bed. Each thought came with an image of my past self and each day I lived in a state of fear.

Coming Out of Addiction

Words have the power to generate great amounts of suffering and when ignored can control us. I didn't think I was ignoring my circumstances, which were so deeply ingrained they were simply a part of me. My pain was on automatic pilot and in control of me until I began applying self-care to my routine. In choosing to peel back our underlayers, the rawer we become.

As a kid and as a teenager, I was unaware of the degree of my emotional turmoil. Later, from the age of 19 through 27, I began drinking a lot more, and that was added to all that stayed covered up. I did not begin mourning my emotions until after the drinking stopped—mourning as though there had been a death.

The first 10 months after the whiteout were among the best of my life. I had never felt as free and alive before that. It was not until the end of the whiteout year that more hidden emotions started to erupt. One day I felt like I was on top of the world, and the next all I felt was ugliness rushing in from every direction. Once that tap was turned on, I couldn't stop it. It spewed out uncontrollably. I went from a whiteout into an emotional shutdown, controlled by all negatively charged beliefs. Looking back on my childhood and teenage years, I see now the level of my anxiety. As the years passed, the underlayers became more exposed, and so did my emotions. Panic attacks grew worse with time, and I felt like I was in a torture box 24 hours a day. I was already taking four to eight sleeping pills per night while drinking, and when I stopped drinking, the pills increased. I took from eight to sometimes 12 or even 14 per night. Because of the panic attacks I began taking anti-anxiety pills as well. When I look back, it's a miracle I didn't overdose.

The whiteout may have taken away my desire to drink (for which I remain grateful), but it did not put the broken pieces of me back together. That would be my responsibility, which I am also grateful. Otherwise, there would have been no journey. Addiction, to me, is a live wire hovering above a burning fire. When we *See It Through*, consciousness fills into the gap where old conditioning once was. Since the past is no longer in charge of us, addiction lets go of us. Addiction is something we think into action, attaching ourselves to and becoming obsessed with a reel to the point where the reel spins us. We no longer must think about drinking to drink, it becomes a reflex.

It was during the second year of the relationship with my husband, Chris, and our first year of marriage, that I not only made the conscious decision to want to feel better mentally but act upon it. I was sober for almost four years when we first met but I was nowhere near feeling mentally well and still reeling on an emotional roller coaster.

I had been in several relationships before Chris but had never felt compelled to address my insecurities. Before Chris, I attracted men as emotionally stunted as I was. Some appeared to have their lives in order, but on the inside, they too were spinning out of control. By the laws of cause-and-effect, we cannot be with anyone who is not inspiring or triggering us to "sea" our feelings. If you think your partner is the crazy one in the relationship, it may be time to look in the mirror.

I pulled Chris into my life, and he pulled me into his because both of us sincerely wanted to change how we felt. The universe works with what we are truthfully thinking and not what we are pretending to think. The two of us came together to work our way out of all that no longer served us well. As willing participants, we both were able to work at it in an atmosphere that was safe. And it was not always an easy road. There were many ups and downs along the way. Our relationship journey could easily extend into its own book, and so I will leave it here for now.

I told myself the reason I made friends with boys while growing up was because I was a tomboy. In truth, it was because I believed women would hurt me. My fear of women attracted other hurt women who wanted to hurt me. Not because they consciously wanted to cause pain, but because that is what I pulled out of them and what they pulled out of me. It's what we all supportively activate behind the scenes. We support one another's ability to "sea" the unseeable in ourselves. We are confronted by certain individuals because, in hindsight, a part of us is ready to venture into what they project. Some of us see it and take advantage of the opportunity, and some of us do not.

It's important to grasp the knowingness that we do not make people do bad things to us. This notion can be extremely threatening to anyone not in agreement with this broader perspective. No one is obliged to do anything they do not want to do. As said in the introduction, this book is not a telling—it is a sharing.

I have already mentioned we enter this life with an already indoctrinated script that pulls to it that which it is and not, who we believe we are today.

Mother

We need not intentionally go out of our way to invite something precarious into our life. It is already being played out by us and picked up by similar frequencies. When I pulled hurt women to me, the ignorant part of me needed them to show me my hurt. In my mind, I was jealous of other women, terrified they would try and take away the men I chose to be with. But not once did I stop to think about what was really going on inside me. I was not actually jealous—that was the guise hiding the real terror. I wanted to feel love toward them. I wanted more than anything to have a bond and a connection with women, yet I was oblivious to everything and felt threatened by them instead. The thought of letting a woman get close to me made my skin crawl.

I asked to sleep with my mother only once as a child and had crawled into her bed. "As long as you stay on your side of the fucking bed you can," she said. I accidentally rolled over to her side, my leg touching hers, provoking her to say loudly, "Get your disgusting fucking leg off of mine!" The word "disgusting" stayed with me until my 40s. Anyone who wanted to get close to me, man or woman, made me feel repulsive. The reel took over and projected the words. Why on earth would anyone want to get close to me? If only you knew what was hiding here underneath these sheets called skin, you too would be repulsed.

Without our knowing, our scripts play out their stories behind the closed doors of our minds and, over time, we add our age-defying insecurities, victimizations, and other ill views of ourselves. That we then throw onto the environment, which brings it back to us through a variety of people, places, and situations. We are not here to get away from ourselves but to get into ourselves and do it through one another.

My mother telling me my touch was disgusting was her answering my crib memory's outgoing call. Confirming and reinforcing the belief that I was too disgusting to want to be picked up. The program reeled out to my childhood and later, adult life. Just like how from the same memory, my brain downloaded all the feelings in combination with the physical pain of my skin hurting.

When Abby passed and I felt abandoned, it triggered all the same feelings and others underneath those feelings, like guilt, regret, and terror—the latter being the most overwhelming. My brain froze the trauma from one time zone and passed it onto several others until it was remembered and *seen through*. Before that, the memory was hidden from me and had more control over me in ways I couldn't see but felt emotional turmoil from none the less.

As I grew up, my mother was always late for everything, which was embarrassing for me. She was always late because she was controlled by a tormented, painful past that frightened her. The past pulled her backwards, making her feel she could never get ahead of it. This gave her anxiety, stole her breath, and made her feel exhausted, which is the reason she slept so much. She wanted to sleep her pain away, but from the moment she got out of bed in the afternoon, it was always there. It was still in charge of her while she slept and she never felt rested.

Her past put her in a constant state of fight or flight, making her body and mind run on all cylinders. I share this part of my past not to have you hate my mother but to help awaken you from your own slumber. You might then see how when you tell your sad stories and do nothing to heal them. They can take control and make you a victim. That energy, in turn, can and will pull toward it more ways to make you feel victimized.

I offer a glimpse of what I once believed was a horrible past and, in doing so, may help you to "sea" out yours. Take a moment now to reflect. Are you currently clinging to a negative past? The ghost is conniving and manipulative and wants to stay a victim, as that is its job to show us only the negative side of the battery. The problem that sometimes spirals out is that it does its job almost too well. Some of us become so spellbound by the negative end that we forget to remember our point of power is in this time zone and when recognized, aligns the positive to negative.

Some say that love moves faster than the speed of light and that the same theory applies to our thoughts. But since all thought is conflicted when in ghost, it moves at a snail's pace. When being conditional, it is impossible to know love. Time goes by fast to the uneducated mind—a mind that thinks is a mind that ticks. The more we try to get through our day, the slower it seems to go. But it is that same unaware thinking that makes it speed up and pass us by. We are not really looking at the day as it happens. Instead, we look ahead at the days to come. Think of standing in the security line at the airport about to miss a flight and the line will not budge. Our insides (reptilian brain that's governing your heart rate, digestion, and respiratory system) speed up, but the outside world feels like it's not moving.

Self-love dissolves all laws and, therefore, has no force so it has no speed. Life does not simply pass us by, giving us the lazy excuse (like there's any other kind) to ask, "where did all the time go?" We feel still in life's line because we are self-caring our way through it. This is how we move through life and not become exhausted by it. This is the embodiment of the endless beginning, moving harmoniously through you. Time, when we are standing in it, falls away, and in its place is the endless beginning.

So, yes, time speeds up in a linear sense, but behind that veil is absolute stillness. Jesus said, "If those who seek to attract you say to you: 'See, the Kingdom is in heaven!' then the birds of heaven will be there before you. If they say to you: 'It is in the sea!' then the fish will be there before you."[2]

If you are someone who right now is feeling that your life is passing you by, it may be time for you to SIT upright (when we act like victims, we stand like how a number seven stands, bent) but don't take my word for it. It must come from you (if, that is, you want it to stick). We all come from a past that will inevitably, and co-creatively, play itself out as a means for us to know ourselves better. You do not make me feel something I don't already feel, and when I blame you for it, I remain hypnotized by the story and cannot move through the emotion. With deflection, there is no self-reflection.

Words like "I need my mother to pay for what she did," or, "Just because she was abused doesn't mean that she had the right to abuse me," are slave programs we succumb to through time. They are excuses we choose to become addicted to by not seeing our way through them, and, inevitably, life passes by us. When we stay stuck in mourning, we are passed from one reel to the next for what feels like forever. The reels appear to fly by, but the leftover feelings move painfully slowly.

Closing, Not Ending

My mother is not just anyone—she is someone I love deeply who instilled in me that which was instilled in her. Today, I realize when I was growing up that my mother simply did the same thing her mother did and what her mother's mother had done. They repeated the same script by reacting to it, minus *Seeing it Through*, which was not a bad thing by definition. Those oblivious reactions served a purpose that ultimately led to a purpose in me. We all worked together to build a movie that would, in time, create a knowing that would rewrite our ancestral history.

My mother, along with all our ancestors, were the bricklayers to the crucial foundation needed for all of us to exist together in timelessness. My grandmother and great grandmother need not be alive and here for me to bring them to life, as I know that all life breathes inside of my thinking them into existence. Everything out there reflects as much. Their faces, although they may already be gone, will be seen in the faces of other people. Until I heal the thrown mother image inside of my head, I'll keep seeing her in other women everywhere I go.

Mother

If I were to have had children, I too may have passed the baton (DNA script) onto them, if not so coincidentally: the family name train stops here. This is not to suggest we all need to come to the end of the line to alter it, but that is how it worked out for me.

To shine light, as well as perspective, on what I said at the beginning of the chapter, sharing our past with one another is what can inspire those around us to be seen freely. Stories are the vessels that carry our learning here. They are the bodies of work that initially, and purposely, render us powerless so that we want to take people's power from them (reel co-creation). When we are ready to "sea" it, it bonds us together (real co-creation). Behind each one of them (emotion) is the seat of our Soul's evolution (waterfall).

This is a sharing of how easy it can be to miss and misinterpret what goes on behind the scenes behind the astral eye with the will only to survive not thrive. When we lock ourselves into that anaerobic hallway, it is only because we have chosen not to "sea" the darker light in us through to its other side. The side, when in combination with its darker self, reveals our light-bringer self. When we choose (it is always a choice) to forget that priceless piece of knowing in ourselves, we can never forgive what we tell ourselves is not forgivable in others.

We can never move on from the past while we believe it controls us. When we give our power to another and refuse (hold a grudge) to take it back (SIT), it ends up crushing us with the weight of eight billion other people's hurt because we are all one mind. No matter where we go in the world, we will be standing with ourselves. If we remember this time zone, we will find our feet. The script is in the driver's seat only when you have fallen asleep. SIT-ting upright opens the box and with it, the entire universe. Remember your royalty, your crown, and your inner, God-given seat at the throne of thrones that connects us to all life, because that life is yours!

I do not forgive my mother for something that I think she did or did not do for or to me.

I extricate the program called mother from my being.

I absolve myself from any further blame for a fault or wrongdoing, especially after the conscious SIT I have revealed. I set myself free from blame, guilt, or responsibility to suffering. And, in the process, without having to do so, I forgave my mother.

I do not draw in the same relationships with women that I did in the past. Today, I can honestly and proudly say that I have loving and supportive relationships with women and men. Not because I have that with my mother, but because I have it with myself.

Why kick off a memoir with what many would consider the start of a life when it can be what supportively closes it? If we are not able to close our life book on a soaring vibrational note, what we are saying is that we have learned nothing. We don't find joy by trying to look beyond something but discover it by splitting ourselves in half. Scripture says that "Behold, the Kingdom of God is within you, and it is outside of you." Jesus said, "Split a piece of wood and I am there; lift the stone and you will find me there."[3]

Heaven is not above hell. It is inside of it! For us to know heaven, we must break through the bottom of hell (Soul Center). And when we "sea" that through, heaven and hell, black and white, you and me, come together as one.

Everything in life takes getting used to. But when we apply ourselves to what makes us feel better, lack alchemizes into abundance. Life is not going to bring you happiness. You must bring it to yourself. Accountability with action means you must take action. When you genuinely want to feel better, you find a way, which is what some of you are doing now in reading this book.

Accountability with action is crucial for my overall wellbeing. I was not able to let go of issues with my mother until I rewrote my childhood. There were many things I tried before then, but none truly worked. There was always a lingering resentment within me and, when she did something to trigger it, I released an all-consuming anger inside myself. Rewriting my childhood opened the door for me to be able to listen and be in my body, which led to me knowing the SIT methods. These four tools have allowed me to be with myself. They have changed my life in the most profound ways, which is why I share them with you now.

This book has been compiled with the knowing that there is no real end— only an endless beginning, and so I close rather than end it. Many of us want to bookend our lives with a beginning and an end. But that is what keeps the astral mind afloat. That is what holds us prisoner! There is no real ending in you and, therefore, no real ending out there. There is only a beginning and the more you choose to self-care your way into remembering that the less you will suffer. Why end this book, or any book, when each is a continuation of something? Your mind, like all minds in accordance with real time, will be forever unraveling itself from this moment on, no matter how hard you try to knot it up in reel time.

ENDNOTES

1   Melinda Ratini. "What to Know About Calcification of the Pineal Gland." WebMD, June 23, 2021. https://www.webmd.com/sleep-disorders/what-to-know-about-calcification-of-the-pineal-gland.

2   Jean Doresse, *The secret books of the Egyptian Gnostics: An introduction to the Gnostic Coptic manuscripts discovered at Chenoboskion*, Viking/Hollis & Carter, New York/London, 1960.

3   The Kingdom among You: Luke 17:21, 2000; "Gospel of Thomas - Marquette University." Accessed July 21, 2022. https://www.marquette.edu/maqom/Gospel%20of%20Thomas%20Lambdin.pdf. .

Made in the USA
Coppell, TX
19 January 2023

11355281R00134